Bed Arrest, the Punishment for BDSM Enthusiasts

By Phil G.

Copyright (C) 2014

ISBN-13: 978-1484091210
ISBN-10: 1484091213

Erotic BDSM Books - Your Erotic BDSM Book Publisher
EroticBDSMbooks.com

Two free bonus books are also included (making this book a $20.85 value!) Your books are presented in this order:

Other books by EroticBDSMBooks.com Include:

*BDSM Master/slave Contract
*Mistress/slave BDSM Contract
*The Absolutely Essential Book of BDSM and S&M Rules
*Things To Do During 3 Hours of Sex; A Step-by-step Guide
*Playtime At The Dom Den; A Step-by-step Guide
*The Absolutely Essential Guide to Great BDSM and S&M Sex
*The Absolutely Essential Dominant/submissive Playtime Experience
*The Absolutely Essential BDSM Sexual Experience
*The Ultimate Collection of S&M and BDSM Rules For Female Submissives and Slaves
*Master and submissive or slave BDSM Contract
*Have Awesome BDSM Sex
*Spanking Dictionary
*Spanking Contract
*BDSM Rules
*Bed Arrest, the Punishment for BDSM Enthusiasts

Book #1
The Spanking Dictionary

Caution is always advised in anything related to spanking, discipline and punishment. Always stay within legal boundaries.

Spanking pronouns, (which include names of spanking websites, spanking actors/actresses, spanking parties and spanking media) are NOT included in this dictionary due to space limitations. **Spanking of minors is not discussed in this book nor advocated**.

ADULT SPANKING - Spanking taking place among and between people who are of legal age.

ADULT SPANKING SCENARIOS - Spanking activities that take place among adults. These are often thought up and set up ahead of time.

AMATEUR SPANKING – (1) Unless a person is spanking, or receiving spankings for money or other material gain (such as Spanking Therapists and professional FemDoms do,) then this category includes most in the adult spanking world. (2) While not all agree on this angle of the definition, it has been used to imply a spanker or spankee who is not proficient in the spanking arts.

ANAL EXAM – The dominant spends a lot of time inspecting, testing and ultimately using the spankee's anus for his/her pleasure.

ANGER MANAGEMENT THERAPY SPANKING - Spanking can be used as a kind of therapy to help manage anger. There are two different approaches.

(1) The angered/stressed person is the spankee and gets spanked for a length and an intensity that allows the anger/stress to be released. Multiple spankings may be needed.

(2) The angered/stressed person is the spanker and spanks for a length and an intensity that allows the anger/stress to be released. Multiple spankings may be needed.

ANNIVERSARY SPANKING - Like birthday spankings this involves a tradition where as part of the festivities one or multiple participants spank and/or get spanked. It may include a special sexual scenario also. Spankophiles might want to get creative and have these anniversaries occur on other anniversaries such as when the couple met, became engaged and/or had their first date.

AVERAGE SPANKING (An) – Your basic everyday spanking, the usual. (Yawn.)

BARE BOTTOM SPANKINGS – Applying the spanking directly to the uncovered buttocks.

There are advantages to this versus spanking the covered buttocks:

1) Better access; the spanker may wish to use the spankee's bottom for other types of stimulation including anal and vaginal stimulation. The spanker may want to rub the naked bottom sensually at various times, etc.

2) Humiliation; the spankee must expose him/herself.

3) Intensity; clothing can lessen the impact of the blows and thus lessen the spanking's sensation and/or ability to provide punishment.

4) Safety; All parties can see how the buttocks is fairing from the blows. Perhaps the intensity needs to be lessened; you might not know if the buttocks are covered.

BARE BOTTOM BEATING – See Bare Bottom Spankings.

BATHBRUSH – A long handled brush used for washing one's self during bathing. It can be an effective spanking tool.

BEDROOM TIME – Being banished to the bedroom after, and/or as part of a punishment spanking. Often this bad girl will get spanked more than once while serving bedroom time.

BED ARREST – A type of BDSM punishment. See the last enclosed book: "Bed Arrest, the Punishment for BDSM Enthusiasts".

BEDTIME SPANKING – (1) Spankings irregularly administered as foreplay to sex prior to going to sleep for the night. (2) Spankings which are administered nightly (or irregularly) when the spankee and/or spanker goes to bed, whether there is to be sexual activity or not.

A number of spankees claim a bedtime spanking helps make them sleepy.

BEHAVIOR MODIFICATION SPANKING – Spanking(s) administered to change unwanted behavior. Repeated and hard spankings may well be necessary to make this work.

BELT – It holds a man's pants up and is a nasty spanking implement. You're in for it now young lady!

BIRCHING – Birching is to spank using a tied together collection of thin tree switches. A nice touch is to have the spankee go out and pick the tree switches herself and tie them together securely for future use or use as soon as it is made.

BIRTHDAY SPANKING - A "traditional" birthday spanking is given on the birthday of the spankee. The formula is to administer one swat for each year of age, plus one additional swat "to grow on, one to live on, one to be happy on, to get married on, etc." The last swat can be the hardest as it's for any bad behavior that he/she did last year.

Spankee beware! Many will say that each birthday party attendee gets to give the same number of spanks, which can make for hundreds of spanks!

The spankee might pick and choose who gets to do the spanking and birthday spankings are typically done clothed as it's often done at children's parties.

Birthday spankings are usually done by hand but if it involves consenting adults spanking that often won't be the case.

Dominants may want to incorporate "practice birthday spankings" with their submissives as another excuse to spank.

Birthday spankings can be given belatedly but typically are for only the spankee's previous birthday (not all his/her birthdays.)

Blindfolding the adult spankee might be a nice touch.

A "Reverse Birthday Spanking" is when the person having the birthday gets to give the spankings instead!

BOARD OF CORRECTION – Slang name for a paddle.

BOTTOMS UP – While more known as a saying for drinking everything from a glass (container) so the bottom of the container is pointing up (thus sending all the liquid into your mouth,) this also means presenting a bottom for a spanking.

BOTTOM RAKING - Sliding your fingernails over and across the spanked or unspanked ass. This should not be done hard enough to puncture the skin or even take any layers of skin off. This should also only be done over the fleshy part of the buttocks and not near the anus or sexual organs.

BROKE THE PADDLE ON MY BUTT – This saying can be put in different ways. It's a source of pride for the spankee that when someone spanked his/her butt using a paddle, the paddle broke upon hitting his/her butt.

BRUTAL SPANKING – See Severe Spanking.

CAPSAICIN CREAM – (Results vary from individual to individual.) - Applying a very small amount of this cream onto the naked buttocks is an alternative to spanking (thus is called "Silent Spanking"). It seeps into the bottom and often is painful. A surprisingly small amount is needed. Make sure to quickly wash your hands after applying it or you will be in pain too. (Better yet use something else to apply it with.)

Rub the capsaicin cream in well. It might take some time to make its impact well noticed. Spankers I suggest you first experiment by rubbing a tiny bit into your spankee's butt. Only drops of it would be necessary to first test his/her resistance to it. Olive oil or vegetable oil can help dissipate the pain. This cream may look innocent but the stuff is evil! (Tiger Balm is another possible punishment cream.) Do not put any of this on or in the anus or vagina!

CANING – This is when a cane is applied with force to the buttocks of the spankee. The cane can hurt more than many other spanking implements due to its smaller surface area so caution is advised. Also see Switching.

CARPET BEATER – A long handled housekeeping tool used to beat dust off of hanging rugs and to spank worthy bottoms.

CHARITY SPANKING - Charity Spanking is when people are spanked in exchange for others sponsoring them and giving money to one or more charities for each good spank they take. Also see Professional Spanking.

CLENCHING – (Clenching Cheeks) – This is when the spankee tightens his/her buttocks muscles together forcefully. This might be done in an attempt to dull the sting of the spanking.

COMING BACK IN FROM THE PUBLIC SPANKINGS – After the spankee returns to a private secluded setting, after having been in the public (and that includes having been to work or having been shopping), she gets a spanking as a natural course of events. This is over and above any other spankings she's getting for any other reason. This is associated with but the opposite of Going Out in the Public Spanking.

CONFESSIONAL {THERAPY} SPANKING - (1) A religiously related spanking scene where the spanker plays an authoritative person of religious faith who spanks the spankee in an effort to get him/her to be more religiously righteous or pay for his/her sins. This may be more popular in Domestic Discipline households. (This happened for real a lot more in centuries past than most hear about.)

(2) The spankee perhaps was raised in a strict religious environment and needs that type of strict (and perhaps regular) guidance to stay on the straight and narrow. A good spanking once or twice a week for just this could be a pleasant addition to your relationship. This obviously has similarities to the confessional of Catholics and doing penance.

(3) In an attempt to get the spankee to confess to something, he/she is spanked. Once he/she confesses then punishment would be administered, which would be another type of spanking such as Punishment Spanking.

CONFIDENTIAL SPANKING – The spanking partners agree to keep their spanking relationship and other spanking related activities secret, except to whom they both agree on. It is essential to follow this rule.

CONSENSUAL SPANKING – Informed and agreed-upon spanking that takes place between and among consenting adults.

CORPORAL PUNISHMENT – This is physical punishment inflicted on the human body. This includes spanking but can also include the death penalty.

CROP – A slapping instrument originally meant to urge horses to move. It can be a wonderful spanking implement.

CRUEL TO BE KIND – A saying that is loosely associated with the potentially beneficial impact of adult spanking.

DETENTION ROOM – This is where many naughty schoolgirls go in spanking films and fantasies. This is the location of much discipline, primarily spanking.

DISCIPLINE - It incorporates punishment to correct disobedience of the rules and/or other unacceptable behavior.

DIZZY SPANKING - For this kind of spanking, the spankee is spun around on foot or in a chair that can spin around, until he/she is dizzy. The spankee is then spanked. This is for healthy spankees only and it's essential to take care for safety.

DOMESTIC DISCIPLINE – (Christian Domestic Discipline, Spanking for Jesus, Loving Domestic Discipline) – This typically is discipline relegated for couples, and often is administered in Christian dominated households. Rules are instituted and penalties for disobedience are administered. The male tends to be the dominate person (Head of Household [HOH]).

DOMINATION SPANKING – The spanking often includes additional aspects of domination such as oral commands, punishment and physical restraint.

DROPSEAT PAJAMAS – These pajamas open at the buttocks for excreting waste and spanking.

DUEL SPANKING - (Tandem Spanking) - This is a Spanking Contest between spanking couples. The spanking is done simultaneous or one at a time. See Spanking Contest.

ENDURANCE SPANKING - This can be done to determine the spanking length and intensity limits of a spankee. (Of course limits change with time.) How much can the spankee take, how many swats, how hard can the swats be, how long can the spanking go on? Are there certain spanking implements that the spankee doesn't do as well with?

Spanking models often go through this unless they have good references.

ENEMA SPANKINGS – Combining enemas with spankings. The spankee is given a spanking then an enema is administered. The spankee releases the water and immediately gets another spanking.

EROTIC SPANKING - Erotic Spanking are spanking activities and techniques that are executed expressly to enhance sexual pleasure. Admittedly spanking (even the thought of spanking) likely enhances a spankopile's pleasure but with Erotic Spanking it's taken a step further. For instance the couple can alternate spankings with the use of a variety of sexual toys and/or manual sexual stimulation.

The spankee can be securely tied down so she/he is immobile and can be enjoyed in other ways after and in-between spankings.

EXERCISE SPANKING – If the spankee needs motivation to exercise and/or exercise harder, spanking can be of use. The spankee can be spanked whenever exercise goals are not reached and/or can get the more desirable reward of a pleasurable spanking when the goals are met.

EXHIBITION SPANKING – This is when spanking models, professional or amateur, provide the public with a spanking related show. The spankee(s) could be clothed or exposed. Also see Public Spanking.

EXORCISM SPANKING – ("Exorcism Beating") - This occurred historically in various places and times in both western and eastern orthodox Christianity, as well as in other religions. This also occurred as part of the inquisitions. In most cases however, the spankee was lucky if their main punishment was only being spanked (beaten.)

Over the centuries some clergy members, particularly those that still were allowed to have sex, set up chambers where women were spanked, sometimes on a sizable wooden cross, for their purported transgressions. It might have been just one spanking or a semi-regular occurrence.

The spankee's buttocks may or may not be exposed for the beating and onlookers may or may not be allowed to watch, or even aid in the beatings.

F/f SPANKING – Female spanking female.

F/m SPANKING - Female spanking male.

FIFTY SHADES OF GREY - A groundbreaking, famous 2011 erotic romance novel by British author E. L. James. Its erotic scenes include BDSM activities such as bondage, discipline, dominance/submission, sadism and masochism.

FIRM HAND – The spanker has a strong and likely big hand that can deliver impressively hard spanks.

FLOGGING – A flogger is a variation of the cat-of-nine-tails whip. It's typically made of suede or real leather and has many individual elastic strands attached to the handle.

GOING OUT IN THE PUBLIC SPANKING – Before the spankee goes out into the public (and that includes going to work or shopping), she gets a spanking as a natural course of events. This is over and above any other spankings she's getting for any other reason. This is associated with Coming Back in from the Public Spankings.

GOOD OLD FASHION SPANKING – These are the standard spankings we grew up with. Silent Spankings and many if not all spankings when the spanker is tied down to spanking furniture, likely are not in this category. This term denotes a hard or harder than normal spanking.

GROUP SPANKING – When a multiplicity of people conjugate for the expressed purposes of engaging in one or more kinds of spanking and spanking related endeavors.

HALLOWEEN SPANKING – Spanking on Halloween while people are in costume. Ideally the spankee(s) should not know who's doing the spanking. Another version has it that the spankee(s) are the ones that people can't tell the identity of.

HAIRBRUSH – (Hated Hairbrush) – The household hairbrush makes a very effective and surprisingly intense spanking tool. Mmmmmm!

HAND SPANKING – Directly applying the spanking blows to those naughty butt cheeks with your hand(s).

HANDPRINT – On a well spanked red ass, if the spanker lands a single hard spank, a white handprint on the otherwise red ass cheek might appear for a short time.

HARD SPANKINGS – A true spankophile should be able to take a hard spanking, at least from time to time. Hard spankings might only be relegated for punishment. Technically a hard spanking should not have the intensity of a severe spanking. Depending however on the pain threshold level of the spankee, a hard spanking could make a spankee cry.

Hard spankings however may evolve into your norm. You may find it best to tie down the spankee for a hard spanking.

The spanker can make demands of the spankee during a hard spanking, demands that need to be promised to be met before the spanking can stop. Perhaps by using a vibrator in her anus she would be required to cum before the spanking could stop.

Unless the spankee has very developed resistance, his/her bottom should be red and perhaps marked from a hard spanking.

If the spankee is female it's suggested that no hard spanking ever ends unless her pussy is wet just from the spanking and she's promising to be a very good girl!

HEATING PAD – (1) After a good spanking, if additional punishment is warranted, laying the heated pad over the well spanked buttocks might be the answer. (2) The spankee could place his/her butt on the heating pad before the spanking possibly making it more tender. (3) For some sitting on the heating pad can feel like punishment.

HOLIDAY SPANKING – Spankings in some cases can really add to the holiday cheer! (Of course there's always Spanking Santa in his red outfit!)

HOT SPANKING – Spanking that are more sexually stimulating than most.

HOUSE PADDLE – A paddle that is kept readily available as a courtesy for guests to use. (It can be another spanking implement instead and named accordingly).

HUMILIATION THERAPY SPANKING – Sometimes a person needs more humility, one way to give him or her more humility is to combine domination with long, hard spankings. Or just a long hard spanking could do the trick. Spanking Therapists and FemDoms can specialize in this.

ICE SPANKING – There are variations to this spanking technique. If you're interested you and your partner should experiment and find the way that works best for you.

The spankee will need to have her buttocks fully exposed. The spanker can do any of the following, or combine them:

a) First rub ice on/across her naked buttocks until the ice has melted. Dry the spankee's buttocks if so desired and administer a good spanking to the spankee.

b) After the first spanking is completed, start over with more ice and repeat this until you're done.

IF-THEN – This scenario can be used with adults, particularly in Domestic Discipline relationships. The number of spankings, spanking duration, intensity, length, implement used and number of spankings the spankee gets are set up ahead of time for a wide range of infractions. Over spending on a credit card would have a clear and previously defined punishment, as would being late for work etc. Couples can spend a lot of quality horny-time determining what punishments the submissive member of the relationship would get for which infraction.

IMPULSE SPANKING – Unexpectedly administering a spanking without warning and perhaps for no particular reason.

INSUFFICIENT DISCIPLINE – When the submissive party thinks (to him/herself, or out-loud) that the dominant is not disciplining him/her adequately or is strong enough emotionally to administrate the discipline.

JUICY BUTT – A bottom that likely is great for spanking (or one that someone thinks would be great for spanking.)

KNEADING (aka Petrissage) - The palms of the hands and/or fingers work the buttock's muscle and fat tissue. Kneading a spankee's bare buttocks is also popular before, during, and/or after a spanking.

KNICKERS DOWN – An English saying meaning "panties down" in preparation for the spanking she so desperately needs.

LEATHER BUTT - A slang term for buttocks that are comparatively insensitive to spanking and do not mark easily. With enough spankings many buttocks become less sensitive.

LESBIAN SPANKING – When women play with each other sexually, and that includes spanking.

LESBIAN SPANKING STORIES – Erotic girl-girl spanking literature.

LIMIT – The point where the submissive party is unwilling to accept any spanking related additional intensity, duration and/or experience.

LINGERIE SPANKING – Spanking while the pretty lady is wearing lingerie.

M/f SPANKING – Male spanking female.

MOTIVATIONAL SPANKING – This type of spanking scenario can help the spankee reach their goal. Perhaps the goal is good grades in college, or additional weight loss, or quitting smoking. Motivational spanking can work (but like anything in life is not guaranteed to work.)

(1) Before the spankee embarks on their endeavor he/she can be given the first motivational spanking, a hard spanking that really shows him/her that it's better to stick with the program. His/her subconscious mind needs to be motivated and a really good spanking might do just that.

(2) Should the spankee fail to reach previously established goals, he/she should be very soundly spanked and otherwise punished. Other punishments can include corner time, not being allowed to wear cloths (when in private,) Bed Arrest, orgasm denial and other forms of humiliation can also be incorporated. Perhaps you'd also like to invite all your kinky friends over to also give him/her a good spanking.

KISS OF THE PADDLE – When a blow from a paddle on the butt leaves a significant mark.

LAP-WRIGGLING SPANKING – (a.k.a. Good Old-fashion Lap-wriggling Spanking) – Wiggling while over a lap getting spanked. (This is more of an English term.) This wiggling likely is because the spanking is particularly intense or the spankee's ability to take a spanking is not too developed.

LIGHT SPANKING – This can be applied to a clothed or bare bottom. It can be administered by hand or via the use of a spanking implement. It should not be particularly painful for most spankees.

LONG, HARD SPANKING – A lengthy and intense punishment spanking meant to change unacceptable behavior.

MAINTENANCE SPANKINGS – (Preventative Maintenance Spankings) - Spankings administered on a regular basis to keep the spankee on the straight and narrow. Punishment spankings are administered in addition to these.

MARATHON SPANKING – Lengthy spanking sessions that might be part of spanking contest or simply for a couple to establish their own personal best. In some marathon spanking sessions the couple can take a short break periodically.

MARKS – (Spanking Marks) – A good spanking with more than moderate intensity (depending on how sensitive the spankee's bottom is) can leave the bottom a lovely shade of red. It also can leave light contusions and more significant bruises. These bruises (aka "marks") could remain for days or longer or they can be gone in hours. A spankophile is proud of these marks hence the phrase "wears her (his) marks with pride".

MEMORY RECOVERY SPANKING – Spankings administered to hopefully help the spankee remember things he/she had forgotten. The hope is that he/she can remember that forgotten thing while being spanked or afterwards.

MODERATE INTENSITY SPANKING – A spanking administered with only moderate intensity typically will give the bottom some or more redness. It shouldn't make the spankee cry or leave marks. This all depends on how sensitive the spankee's ass cheeks are.

MOTIVATIONAL SPANKING – This type of spanking scenario can help the spankee reach their goals. Perhaps the goal is good grades in college, or weight loss, or quitting smoking. Motivational spankings can work (but like anything in life is not guaranteed to work.)

(1) Before the spankee embarks on their endeavor he/she can be given the first motivational spanking, which is a serious spanking that really show him/her that it's better to stick with the program. His/her subconscious mind needs to be motivated also and a really good spanking might do just that.

(2) Should the spankee fail to reach previously established goals, he/she should be very soundly spanked and otherwise punished. Other punishments can include corner time, not being allowed to wear cloths (when in private,) Bed Arrest, orgasm denial and other forms of humiliation can also be incorporated. Perhaps you'd also like to invite all your BDSM/kinky friends over to give him/her a spanking.

MUSICAL SPANKING – Spanking to the beat of the music and/or for the length of the musical composition. (Ever spanked to "Bolero"?)

Another great thing about music is that it might cover up the sound of the spanks hitting the spankee's bottom and noises the spankee utters as his/her bottom is reddened.

NAKED SPANKING – The spankee, and optionally the spanker, are not wearing any cloths.

NSA SPANKING – (No Strings Attached Spanking) – Casual spanking where a special relationship is not necessary.

OLD FASHIONED BARE BOTTOM SPANKING – These are the standard spankings we grew up with. Silent Spankings and many if not all spankings when the spanker is tied down to spanking furniture, likely are not in this category. This term denotes a hard or harder than normal spanking.

OTK – (a.k.a. OTK Spanking) – Short for Over The Knee. This is one of the most popular spanking positions. Its benefits include that the spanking can start quickly versus having to tie the spankee up. Also the spankee's private parts and ass, with all its features, are in easy reach for the spanker's use (assuming the spankee allows that.)

PADDLE – A rigid spanking implement that typically is quite a bit longer than it is wide. The thickness of a paddle can vary. Paddles can increase the intensity of the spanking blows and make spanking a less tiring affair for the spankers. Paddles are usually made of wood but can be made of other hard materials such as acrylic.

PARTY SPANKING – Spanking that takes place at social gatherings. This includes Spanking Games and Group Spankings. Party Spanking is not the same as Spanking Parties.

PLAYFUL SPANKING – This can be when the spankee gets only light to moderate swats or a limited number of quick swats. Consensual playful spankings might be used to break the tension.

POUTING - To make a facial expression that indicates dissatisfaction; sulking. This might be done by the spankee prior to the spanking or when there is an indication that a spanking will take place in the future.

PRIVATE SPANKING - These spankings are given in an isolated private setting with invited company only.

PREVENTATIVE MAINTENANCE SPANKING – See Maintenance Spanking.

PROFESSIONAL SPANKING – When money or material goods are exchanged for one or more spankings. Spankings are given professionally by Spanking Theraphists, FemDoms, Spanking Demonstrators and others. It could also be the opposite where it's the spanking model that gets spanked in exchange for money or material goods. (This includes spanking pictures and spanking video models.) Charity Spanking is when people are spanked in exchange for others giving money to one or more charities for each good spank the spankee takes.

PUBLIC SPANKING – (This includes Exhibition Spanking) – Spankings given in a public or semi public non-group spanking environment. (Not recommended!)

PUNISHMENT AGREEMENT – A Punishment Agreement is an oral or written agreement that defines what punishments will be given for what offenses. See Spanking Contract and BDSM Contract.

PUNISHMENT FETISH – The idea of being punished, or even of being punished in a certain way (such as being spanked) in some way turns on the individual and could be a re-occurring fantasy.

PUNISHMENT ROOM – A room, or area of a room (often the basement, bedroom or the dominant's study) where most of the spankings take place.

PUNISHMENT SPANKING - (Discipline Spanking) – These spankings leave the spankee's bottom red and marked. These are hard spankings meant to change a wayward spankee's behavior. Typically the female spankee (and sometimes male) will cry from these. Also applied as part of the punishment could be corntime, bedroom time and other punishments. Perhaps the spankee will only be allowed to crawl for the rest of the day/night if going somewhere in the house, (obviously privacy is required.) Maybe one punishment spanking will not be enough, or even two! The subconscious mind needs to know what he or she did is no longer allowed!

PURIFICATION RITUAL SPANKING – This spanking category is more on the spiritual side. It can combine enemas, massage, prayer, meditation and/or bathing for spiritual arousal and/or renewal.

PUSSY SPANKING – The vagina is lightly spanked for stimulation and/or punishment.

QUICKIE SPANKING – When time is limited, but the spankee must have a spanking, he/she can be bent over the nearest applicable furniture or go over your lap for an immediate spanking. Often this is when the spankee is already dressed for an occasion. A quickie spanking needs to be given instantly, likely without any significant preparation, waiting time, discussion, or scolding.

REAL TEARS – This indicates that what's occurring is a good hard spanking! Sometimes during a spanking video shoot, the spankee, in-between takes, has a bit of water put by her eyes to mimic tears. No need to do that when the tears are real!

RED BOTTOM SPANKING - (a.k.a. Red Ass Spanking) – A good spanking should leave the spankee with some or more redness on his/her bottom. A bottom that is covered with redness would be from a true Red Bottom Spanking that the spankee can 'wear' with pride! The red bottom may be accompanied with marks (bruises).

RELIGIOUS SPANKING – Religious spanking has a very long history. Men and women's buttocks have been beaten for, and by, religious authorities in many past civilizations. Certain members of Christian clergy are recorded to have spanked (women in particular) back when it was easier for them to get away with it. Inquisitioners would beat men and women, often without mercy, as they considered them to be an affront to god.

A part of religious spanking history that may be of interest is how often women in the medieval and post medieval centuries, (often coupled women,) would request a spanking from the clergy (such as their minister or priest) as atonement for their sins or as confidential punishment for something isolated that they did. Often their husbands okayed it. Heck it was a lot better than going to hell right, at least that was what they thought.

Some church building basements had a separate section for these atonement sessions. This happened more often than people realize.

REWARD SPANKING – (1) When a spankophile just can't get enough spankings that you are actually able to reward her/him by giving a spanking. (2) A FemDom might consider all spankings she gives to her slaves to be a reward, or should be viewed as a reward. Punishment for bad behavior is typically more severe than a reward spanking.

ROMANCE SPANKING - This is for spanking couples involved in a romantic relationship. The spanking can be mixed with sexual stimulation and intercourse.

RULER – (Wooden Ruler) – Though often made of wood, it can be made of other substances. Some rulers are thicker than others and somewhat longer than one foot. The thick 1½ foot ruler is a dandy! The yardstick can be very useful for those long reaches, for instance when the naughty girl is sucking on a man's cock and he wants to spank her at the same time. (Watch out for those teeth!)

SAFE SPANKING – Don't spank too hard. Some spankees' butts are able to take more abuse than others, at least until the butt toughens up (assuming it does.) Also you want all parties to feel secure with the location and privacy of the place selected for the spanking.

SANDPAPER CHAIR – After the spankee is spanked, he or she sits naked on sandpaper. An alternative is to rub sandpaper on the spankee's well spanked bottom and/or run your fingernails over the spanked buttocks.

SCHOOLGIRL SPANKING – The naughty (adult) schoolgirl discipline fantasy is one of the most popular spanking fantasies. She is dressed in the pelted skirt and white dress shirt (perhaps also with a tie) and is constantly getting in trouble so she is constantly spanked! All female spanking enthusiasts (spankees) should have a schoolgirl outfit!

SELF-SPANKING – Spanking yourself.

SEXUAL DOMINATION – (Associated with Sensual Domination) - The dominant person controls and orchestrates the sexual relationship and sexual activity with the submissive person.

SERIOUS SPANKING – (1) Spanking enthusiasts that take the art of spanking seriously. (2) A hard or even severe spanking and typically is reserved for punishment.

SERVANT SPANKING – (Also see Slave Spanking) - Spanking of servants (though in past centuries and millennia they more often were slaves) occurred often. In those days masters and mistresses lorded over their servants with more power than they do today. If the lord (or mistress) of the house thought beating the servant would make good discipline (or simply enjoyed it), that was the servant's fate should she wish to continue working there, or often anywhere else as employment references were important.

The servant girl might be spanked for pleasure by the master of the house. She might be enjoyed in other ways too, though not as often from vaginal intercourse. Servant girls that ended up taking the role of concubines might be treated better and have less mundane work to do. Wives in those days were frigid move often than now. This might be because they were afraid to have too much sex with their husbands as it was so much easier to get pregnant back then thanks largely to a pronounced lack of birth control and the stricter demands of the prevailing religious forces that were staunchly against birth control. (Also women died during childbirth a lot more frequently back then.) A surprising number of wives simply considered the sex demands of their husbands to be too much and welcomed their use of a servant in that manner if it freed them from that arduous duty, (assuming he did not get her pregnant and kept his distance from her emotionally.)

The mistress of the house might order someone to be spanked (beaten) and perhaps do it herself. Husbands and male friends (or other servants) often were happy to do the beating for her, assuming it was a female getting spanked.

The person being beaten may or may not have the area being beaten, fully exposed (thus naked.)

SEVERE SPANKING - This type of spanking can cause much redness and/or severe bruising (marking), blistering or worse on the buttocks of most spankees. The spankee likely will find sitting a challenge for a certain amount of time. This needs to be done in a consensual manner and might not be legal.

SILENT SPANKING – (1) When the spankee is not allowed to utter any noise while being spanked. (2) Alternatives to spanking that quietly give the butt pain, such as the application of capsicum cream (but a very small amount) and the less effective Tiger Balm. Do not put it on the anus or sex organs.

SLAVE SPANKING – See Servant Spanking. (1) In the modern world of BDSM (Bondage, Domination, Sadism and Masochism) the submissive person is called a slave and is under the influence and/or control of the dominate party typically called the "Master" (if male) or "Mistress" if female. The submissive slave is dominated and spanked when the dominant feels it is necessary for discipline and/or pleasure. (2) (See Servant Spanking for more on this part of the definition.) Slaves in ancient times often were considered part of the family. They may have been expressly gotten for purposes of physical and sexual pleasure. They were spanked publically and privately in Roman and Greek locations at the whim of their owners. In the more modern slave ownership period including the Caribbean and in North America, black slave girls would also be used for sexual gratification when their owners wanted it. Also other male slaves might spank other slaves for various reasons, particularly when they were a supervisor.

SLIPPERING - Using a slipper as the spanking implement.

SOOTHING CREAM – (Cold Cream) - A cream applied to a well spanked bottom to limit the sensation of pain.

SOUND SPANKING – See Hard Spanking.

SPANKABLE – (Spankworthy) – The person is well suited to be spanked. They may appear to have an ass, due to its shape and/or appearance, that appears particularly well designed to be spanked. The mannerisms of the person should scream "spank me"! A professional spanking actress should have great "spankability".

SPANKED TO TEARS – When the spankee is spanked hard enough to cry real tears. Bad girl!

SPANKFEST – A synonym for "Spank Feast". This is a gathering, public or private, where spanking is one of the primary events (or at least is publicized to be.)

SPANKING ART - (Spanking Comics) – Spanking themed art.

SPANKING AGREEMENT - An oral or written agreement regarding spanking related activities. See Spanking Contracts.

SPANKING BEGINNERS – Spanking Beginners typically have little or no significant experience with giving a spanking and/or receiving a spanking.

It's important that the beginner's first spanking (or first few spankings) are as positive an experience as possible. Does the spankee want it to be a sexual experience also, if so then make sure sexual stimulation is accented. A bad experience now could turn this person off from spanking and another butt is lost to the spanking world :(

SPANKING BLOG – A (preferably) regularly updated online diary/web magazine that individuals and organizations keep regarding spanking pursuits.

SPANKING BONDAGE - When bondage is included with the spanking. Typically this means that the spankee is securely tied down and immobile for his/her spanking. Perhaps he/she is tied down to a piece of spanking furniture.

SPANKING CLUB – These associations provide a way to meet and/or otherwise intertwine with others in the spanking scene. They're sometimes called "Munches". Spanking clubs have grown quite a bit in number in recent years.

SPANKING CONTEST – When couples compete with spankings for a prize or prizes. The rules vary from contest to contest. Possibly included are:

A) Extra points for the spankee with the reddest butt
B) Extra points for the nicest looking marks
C) Points deducted for blistering or appearance of blood (typically then the spanking is over for them anyway)
D) Extra points for sexiest spankee's behavior while being spanked.
E) Points deducted for the spankee trying to block blows or get away
F) Points deducted for the spanker tiring too quickly
G) Extra points for the spankee with the sexist outfit and/or the outfit most conducive to making the spanking easier
H) Extra points for the spanker/spankee couple that is the most fun to listen to during the spanking
I) Extra points for how sexy and submissive the spankee is during and at the end of the spanking. She will have to beg for forgiveness, etc.
J) Extra points to the couple that uses the most spanking implements during the spanking
K) Extra points to the spankee's bottom that feels the best after being well spanked.
L) Extra points to the spankee that gets the most aroused
M) Extra points for the spankee with the most spanks during that time period.

Multiple spankings can be going on at the same time. Also see Duel Spanking.

SPANKING CONTRACT -It's a good idea for the participants to sit down and talk about their spanking scenarios, including under what circumstances the spanking will take place, how the spanking will be delivered, number of swats, instruments to be used, position of the person to be spanked, whether spanked with clothing on or bare bottom, etc. All participants then have an oral agreement on the terms, or have a signed written contract on the terms. This author sells a Spanking Contract through your bookstore.

SPANKING CURRENCY - This is when spanks take the place of money, more specifically in place of your country's currency. How many spanks do you have in your spanking account? What are you going to buy with them? Or perhaps you are making a trade? Do you have a debt to pay off?

A common "spanking currency" scenario is paying off a debt. The spankee gets spanked in exchange for the debt.

SPANKING DANCE —The sub/slave does a sexy dance in front of her dominant and is spanked at various parts (times) of her dance. Perhaps it's after the end of each song, or if her dancing is not of an acceptable nature.

SPANKING DEMONSTRATION - When spanking partners demonstrate various aspects of spanking, including spanking implements and the best ways to spank.

SPANKING ENTHUSIAST – (Spankophile) - Someone who enjoys spanking, either receiving or giving. This includes activities related to spanking such as spanking media, building spanking furniture and spanking modeling.

SPANKING FANTASY – (Spanking Fantasies) – Mental images that run through one's head associated with spanking. A great many people have these.

SPANKING FOR COUPLES – Adult spanking activities that couples involve themselves in.

SPANKING FURNITURE – These apparatuses are used to place and secure one or more spankees. These include whipping benches, the spanking horse, the birching horse and the spanking bench. The spankee may or may not be tied down to it. The spankee often will find him or herself in the kneeling position or bent-over position. There should be easy access to their buttocks and often spanking furniture make the buttocks the most elevated portion of the spankee's body. Also being able to take and/or play with the spankee sexually while on and/or tied to spanking furniture is of pronounced importance.

SPANKING GAMES – (1) Online interactive games where the players determine who gets spanked and the intensity of the spankings. A spanking game may let the player interactively spank one or more characters. (2) Physical games such as Strip Poker that calls for one or more participants being spanked at various intervals. This type of spanking game typically has a way of determining who the spankee is and who the spanker is.

SPANKING HOST – The host or hostess at spanking social events and online and real-life spanking clubs.

SPANKING IMPLEMENTS – These physical devices are used to aid and enhance the delivery of the spanking blows. Examples include paddles, straps, slappers, floggers, rods, switches, canes, spanksticks, crops, the tawse and whips. Not everybody agrees but some people feel this category also includes restraint aids such as handcuffs and rope.

SPANKING LIFESTYLE – The world of spanking is innately intertwined into the lives of the spanker and/or spankee.

SPANKING MAGAZINE – Content from these wonderful periodicals now are often also online.

SPANKING MASSAGES – Combining full or partial body massages with spankings. The massaging may be the primary activity or vice versa.

SPANKING MASTURBATION – (1) Masturbating during and/or after a spanking and masturbating on those days afterwards while your bottom is still sore from the spanking. (2) Being spanked for masturbating.

SPANKING ORGASM – An orgasm that is obtained while one is being spanked, or while their buttock is still smarting from having been spanked in hours or days since the spanking.

SPANKING PARTY – Spanking parties might be in a home, a hotels or resort and are a gatherings specifically set up to accommodate spanking. Often there tends to be a significantly higher percentage of males at these events than females.

SPANKING POSITIONS – The bodily location of spanker and spankee just prior to, during and just after the spanking.

SPANKING PRACTIONER – See Spanking Enthusiast.

SPANKING REMINDER – This often is a short but relatively intense spanking session to make sure the spankee remembers to be obedient and/or is reminded as to what kind of punishment awaits her should she do something wrong.

SPANKING ROLEPLAY - There are many role-play scenarios that can include spanking. Naughty nurse, submissive maid, naughty schoolgirl, misbehaving cheerleader and warden/prisoner role playing is popular with male dominants and female submissives.

Spanking Roleplaying can require acting and props but it always includes a generous helpings of spankings.

SPANKING SERIES – A sequence and/or collection of spankings and/or spanking characters, stories, videos and/or pictures, which have certain characteristics in common.

SPANKING SESSION – Most associated with visits to FemDoms and Spanking Therapists. These are often "visits" that have a purpose but it still can be just a girlfriend and boyfriend meeting for fun.

SPANKING STICK – These look a lot like manmade canes.

SPANKING STORIES – (Spanking Novels, Spanking Novellas, Spanking Series, Corporal Punishment Fiction, Flagellation Erotica, Romantic Spanking Stories) – These are literature adventures involving spanking. These go back to the 1700s and may or may not involve sexual activities. The Marquis de Sade is among the most famous of these authors. In the past these tended to be clandestine publications that were sold secretly.

SPANKING THERAPIST – A person that administers Spanking Therapy.

SPANKING THERAPY – This aims to help spankees improve themselves. Perhaps he/she needs more motivation or just the tension release of a good spanking. The spanking is conducted by a professional. The spankee's needs are assessed and addressed in a controlled, nurturing environment (assuming nurturing is what the spankee wants.)

SPANKING VIDEOS – Spanking videos have proliferated with the Internet. As is obvious, these videos show spankees getting spanked and often dominated in other ways.

SPANKING WITH **ANAL STIMULATION** – (1) Directly stimulating the anus while giving a spanking (which can include aiming the blows at the anus and/or to make the blows include the anus.) It can occur before a spanking, and/or in between spankings, and/or after a spanking. This might involve inserting a butt plug (inflatable or otherwise), finger(s), anal vibrator, a dildo, or rectal thermometer into the anus. It might include carefully spanking a dildo that's already put into the anus to make it move up and down in the anus as blows are applied to it and the buttocks. (2) Actually spanking the anus with a narrow spanking instrument. (Spanking related enemas are a separate subject, see Enema Spanking.

Anal stimulation doesn't necessarily include anal intercourse.

SPANKING THE MONKEY – Male masturbation.

SPANKOPHILE – – (aka Spanking Enthusiast) - Someone who enjoys spanking, either receiving or giving. Their interest could also include spanking implements, discussing spanking, spanking media, building spanking furniture and spanking modeling.

SPENCER SPANKING PLAN – A well known domestic discipline spanking contract that originated in the 1930s.

STING AND THUD - Thinner spanking instruments such as switches release their energy closer to the skin and thus 'sting' more. Thicker spanking instruments such as paddles release their energy down further in the buttocks making more of a "thud" sensation.

STRAP – (aka Leather Strap) – A spanking instrument of various sizes that can be deliciously effective. It's often made of leather and thus is pliable.

STRESS RELIEF SPANKING – (Tension Relief Spanking) - The aim of these spankings are to eliminate frustration and guilt and cleanse oneself mentally. At the conclusion of these spankings relaxation and comfort can be had by the spankee.

STRUGGLING – When the spankee fails to hold his/herself adequately in place for/during and after their spanking.

SUBMISSIVE SPANKING – When the spankee wants to feel dominated as part of the spanking, over and above the domination involved with him/her getting spanked.

SUBMIT AND OBEY – A Dom/sub lifestyle outlook where the submissive submits and obeys his/her Dominant.

SWITCH SPANKING – Where the spanker and spankee take turns spanking each other.

SWITCHING – (Associated with Birching) – A switch is a flexible thin branch (rod) from one or more trees. (A collection of thin branches can be tied together to also be used as a spanking implement.) A switch is applied with force to the buttocks of the spankee. The switch like the cane can hurt more than many other spanking implements due to its thinner surface area so caution is advised. Also see Caning.

TENDER – The tendency for the buttocks to become sensitive to the touch after a good spanking.

TENSION RELIEF SPANKING – See Stress Relief Spanking.

THRASHING – This term is more popular in England and denotes a hard spanking/beating often with one or more implements.

TICKLE SPANKING – (1) Tickling the buttocks and then spanking it (an act that can be repeated.) (2) Tickling various parts of a person's body such as their belly and the bottoms of their feet, and also spanking that person's buttocks, alternatively or simultaneously.

TIT WHIPPING – Spanking the breasts of a woman using one or more implements. This can only be done consensually and with caution.

TRADITIONAL SPANKING – This denotes standard methods of spanking. No unusual methods of buttocal pain infliction, such as Silent Spanking, would be included in this category.

TOP UP SPANKING – These are given regularly, even every few days, even in addition to any other spankings the spankee has received. These spankings are for bad behavior that the spankee got away with during that time period (say week) and for bad behavior she might be tempted to do in the following week. See Maintenance Spanking.

TOUCH-YOUR-TOES – When in a standing position the spankee may be ordered to reach down and touch as close to their toes (perhaps their knees) as possible so their buttocks can tighten and stick out thus becoming an easier target to spank.

TOUGHEN-UP SPANKING – These spankings (and spankings in general) if given with regularity, can dull nerve endings in the buttocks as well as toughen tissues in the buttocks. The spankee might evolve into having a "leather butt" which is a butt that can take a disproportionately hard spanking.

WAKE-UP SPANKING – This well helps to wake up sleepy beauty and typically works much better than an alarm clock.

WARM-UP SPANKING - This is a light spanking, often by hand and perhaps on a clothed bottom, before the "real" and more intense spanking begins. Its purpose is to prepare the butt for the coming onslaught.

WEARS HER (HIS) MARKS WITH PRIDE – (Spanking Marks) – A good spanking with more than moderate intensity (depending on how sensitive the spankee's bottom is) can leave the bottom a lovely shade of red. It also can leave light contusions and more significant bruises. These bruises (aka "marks") could remain for days or longer or they can be gone in hours. A spankophile is proud of these marks hence the phrase "wears her (his) marks with pride".

WEIGHT-LOSS SPANKING – If the spankee needs motivation to lose weight, spanking can be of use. The spankee can be spanked whenever weight loss goals are not reached and/or can have the more desirable reward of a pleasurable spanking when the goals are met. Perhaps the spankee should be given a hard spanking just before the diet is to begin to remind him/her what's in store if transgressions occur.

WELL-SPANKED BUTT – A buttocks that has the tell-tale signs of having gotten a good spanking.

WET SPANKING – For this the spankee's butt is made wet. It can also be when the spankee wears something wet that covers her bottom and is spanked over that. This can enhance the pain coefficient.

WHEEL BARROW SPANKING POSITION – The spanker sits up and the spankee lays her hands on the floor directly in front of the spanker. The spankee spreads her legs and brings her ass and legs up over the sitting spanker's lap. Her legs are positioned on each side of his upper torso. Her pussy and anus are spread wide open next to his midsection. Her ass cheeks are on his lap, her spread open pussy lips are facing him.

WHEEL BARROW SPANKING – When the entire spanking is administered with the spankee in the wheel barrow spanking position (see previous definition.)

WHUPPIN – Slang for whipping.

WOODEN SPOON – This kitchen implement can also double as a spanking implement. Bad girl!

The End

Book #2 - Bed Arrest, the Punishment For BDSM Enthusiasts

By Phil G.

Copyright (C) 2014

Bed Arrest, the Punishment For BDSM Enthusiasts

Trust, care, mutual consent, safe sex practices, and general safety are absolute priorities. No matter what it's suggested that you incorporate at least the following into your playtime and lifestyle:

* Don't tie things around someone's neck, and no breath play, period!
* Create a "Safe word" for the submissive to say when (or if) things get too scary.
* Always be careful and take necessary safety precautions when engaging in BDSM activity. Keep proper medical facilities handy.
* Always insure that a bound person has adequate circulation. If the person tied up has to go to the bathroom or has physical problems, that person must be immediately released from bondage.
* Ask about medical issues before playing and adjust your playing activities according to any medical issues.
* Never leave anyone bound and alone.
* Understand what a gagged person sounds like in sexual ecstasy versus in pain.
* Do not play while under the influence of drugs or alcohol.
Always check that your handcuffs and/or lock keys work before playing. If you have to go to the locksmith to get the handcuffs off, it's going to be embarrassing.
* When removing someone from bondage, allow them to move their own limbs.
* If pregnant or ill, check with your doctor before engaging in BDSM related activity.
* Always play within your own skill base and comfort level.

Defining Bed Arrest

Thank you for reading this book, the first book on bed arrest.

This punishment technique can only be used when all parties involved have fully consented to it.

For consistency's sake, this book discusses bed arrest where the punisher is a male master and the person being sentenced to bed arrest is a female submissive or slave. Bed arrest as a punishment can however work just as well in situations when the two parties involved are of the same sex.

I am honored to say that as a master I have incorporated bed arrest into my relationships many times. I have found that it can be a useful tool for changing errant sub/slave behavior.

In this book I'll also make suggestions regarding how (in my opinion) to most optimally carry out the sentence of bed arrest on a sub/slave. Obviously both parties involved can adapt what's in this book to fit their desires, needs and time schedule.

This book also assumes (for all involved) that the sub/slave will accept being put in bed arrest and obey her master's rules associated with it. Obviously if master tells his sub/slave she's just been sentenced to 10 hours house arrest and she points at him and laughs, then master has a problem.

General Definition - Bed arrest is when a master in a BDSM (or related) relationship orders (thus requires) his sub/slave to stay on her bed at all times other than emergencies, and for those additional activities specified. During the time that she is reprimanded to the bed, master may also punish her in other ways such as spanking. He can also play with her, and of course enjoy her sexually.

Bed arrest, as is obvious, is a lot like an adult version of timeout. It doesn't need to be for a longtime; a 30 minute bed arrest session might get the point across just as well. Still all bed arrests sessions are not the same and the sub's restrictions during her incarceration can make all the difference in the world. However beware guys, with her helplessly stuck there, will you be able to resist playing with her all afternoon? (Let's hope she doesn't consider that punishment.)

During bed arrest her freedom can be seriously restricted and she will have time to think about the importance of changing her errant ways.

I gave many 2 day sentences as well as 30 minute sentences. The longest bed arrest sentence I ever given a sub/slave was 4 days. On many occasions I commuted the sentence down because of good behavior, and/or something unexpected came up and/or her sexy begging finally got to me.

Bed arrest in and of itself might not be considered that extreme a punishment. The liberties that the sub/slave loses during bed arrest as well as other punishments she might also experience during that time perhaps can better determine how well she learns her lesson.

1. When to use bed arrest as a punishment. Perhaps your lovely lady has not been reacting well enough to your usual punishments. Perhaps spanking her used to work well as a punishment but now she gets so turned on by it that if anything she'll misbehave to get a good spanking. Finding a new punishment thus has become a necessity.

2. Length of time for putting the sub/slave in bed arrest. Obviously this varies by what extent she needs to be punished and what her and her master's obligations in life are during that time. (Does she have to go to work? Does she have college classes, etc.?)

As she will be allowed out of the bed (and home) for work and other responsibilities, likely that would mean an increase in the length of her sentence as she would be spending less time in bed arrest overall than a sub/slave that could stay around the home all or most of the day.

My experience (and yours may be quite different) is that if the sub/slave has never served a bed arrest, she may have fantasies associated with it.

3. What the sub/slave is allowed to do during bed arrest – How strict and restrictive will her sentence be, at least for the first half or so? Will she need permission to leave the bed for any reason (with the obvious exception of emergencies) including going to the bathroom?

The general rule of thumb is that the less you allow her to do during bed arrest, the more effective the punishment. During the sentence master can progressively give her back more privileges, such as no longer needing permission to go to the bathroom, watch TV, play videogames, watch movies, read books, use the phone, etc. Also was she tied to the bed at all times? Maybe now she can be unbound. (I would strongly suggest that except for emergencies she is never allowed to use the phone during bed arrest.)

My experience is that it's best to start the bed arrest with her having as few privileges as possible and being bound securely to the bed. You then give privileges back as she earns them and/or begs enough for them.

As it's likely you will let her out of the bed to fix meals and do other chores, you'll then need to make sure she's not taking unusually long to do those activities. If so master may want to threaten her with extending her sentence or perhaps another good spanking will take care of that problem.

4. Bondage and blindfolding during her incarceration. Will she be tied up and/or tied to the bed in bondage for a significant amount of the sentence? I would suggest she is and for a substantial amount of time, at least in the first half or more of her incarceration. Blindfolds can help make her feel more isolated and increase the impact of the punishment. Master will probably want to tie her hands in manner so that she **can't** take the blindfold off when she thinks master is not looking, or at least lower the blindfold a bit to look around real quick. Obviously a respectful, well trained sub/slave should not do this but sub/slaves are after all human.

5) Sub/slave needing permission from her master to leave the bed for anything (other than emergencies.) It may seem harsh but my experience is that bed arrest as a punishment works best when to leave the bed for even essential activities, such as going to the bathroom, the sub/slave first needs to have permission from her master. Because of this the master will find that he will need to be in the dwelling and at earshot at all times, just incase, which obviously could be inconvenient for him. With good behavior on her part, this restriction can be lessened.

6) Master will always determine what she does or doesn't wear during the period of bed arrest. *(This is of course is subject to how cold it is, if company shows up and/or if she has to go out of the house for work or other essential activities.)*

During bed arrest, while in private, it's suggested that she not be allowed to wear any clothing.

During the period of her incarceration, also perhaps remove her authority to wear panties while she is out of the house/apartment doing essential public activities such as work and shopping. *(Don't be surprised if she won't go along with this, particularly if it entails doing this at work. If that's the case guys, let it go.)*

7) Pouting, sulking and possibly rebelling by the sub/slave. Master should prepare for his sub/slave to possibly pout, sulk, and as a lengthy sentence progresses, maybe even try to rebel, though hopefully without going too far. Of course the more time master spends with her in bed, playing with her, spanking her, taking her being massaged by her, lying in bed with her, the happier she'll likely be but perhaps the punishment will be less effective, (or perhaps it could have just the opposite effect and be of good benefit).

It's possible that she will rebel to the point that she says she hates you and leaves the house frustrated. It is her right guys and you can't stop her, unfortunately it's likely also a sign of problems in the relationship, and/or a poorly trained sub/slave and/or a sub/slave that simply does not allow herself to be punished with bed arrest, (and/or perhaps other punishments you include during bed arrest.)

Still perhaps she has had a bad experience with bed arrest in the past? That will have to be dealt with in a responsible, respectful manner.

What if she doesn't like bondage and/or blindfolding then either she takes the plunge and lets you do that to her or you don't do those activities.

Perhaps she has obligations that she feels will interfere with the length of her sentence. You would need to let her off for those obligations anyway and perhaps she doesn't understand that.

On the other hand you as master might now find out that she is not a respectful sub/slave, an immature sub/slave and/or too much of a bratty sub/slave and you should find another.

8) Adding more time to her sentence as well as commuting her sentence. The sub/slave should be aware that more time can be added to her sentence. Additionally privileges might not be returned to her as fast during her sentence if she continues to be a bad girl and/or doesn't seem to be learning her lesson.

On the other hand, if she displays a respectful attitude and takes her punishment respectfully then the opposite can occur. Time can be taken off her sentence, and privileges can be returned more quickly during her sentence.

9. How often can we play while she is in bed arrest? Well guys, she's tied up to the bed, naked and blindfolded, good luck keeping your hands off of her! Still the master isn't the one being punished here so his needs and pleasure shouldn't suffer. If he wants his sub/slave to massage him, she should massage him. If he wants fellatio from his sub/slave, by all means get it. If he wants to take his slave, by all means take her. Still it breaks the monotony for her which might not be as conducive to punishment. But it will likely will give her pleasure, make her feel more wanted and loved. Hopefully that won't interfere with her learning her lesson and it might in fact help. Perhaps playing with her later during her incarceration is the better choice, if the master can hold out that long.

Hopefully throughout her sentence she will be on her best behavior in an attempt to get her sentence reduced.

10. What activities can the sub/slave do while she is in bed arrest?

A) Of course her work and parental responsibilities are fully allowed. (If you're living with kids, as you can imagine this punishment could be difficult to perform.)

Still master must watch to make sure she doesn't spend more time than she ordinarily would with her responsibilities. When that's the case her master may wish to add time to her incarceration and/or punish her in other ways.

B) She is required to satisfy her master's sexual desires as always as well as any other activities that can be performed on the bed that she would ordinarily do for her master. This includes massaging her master.

C) Her master perhaps may still also want to punish her in one or more other manners.

11. Privileges that can be taken away from the sub/slave during bed arrest include (depending on circumstances):

*Being able to enjoy video entertainment such as playing video games, watching videos, TV, movies, etc. That can include her favorite programming that would come on during her period of incarceration. (It can be recorded to be watched after her sentence is over.)

*Being able to talk (unless there is an emergency) or she needs permission to do something.

*Being able to use the phone.

*Being able to write things by hand.

*Being able to read for entertainment, such as books.

*Being allowed to have orgasms or otherwise pleasure herself (but dude that's harsh!)

12. Do you close the door on her during her confinement?
No, but it's the master's choice if she's allowed to look at him.

13. How to react to her begging during incarceration. If your sub/slave is adept at begging and if they can be real sexy while doing it, masters may have to ban begging during bed arrest altogether or deal with the horniness that comes with it.

I for one like it when she begs and you can require a certain number of "begs" from her before you'll even consider commuting her sentence.

14. Additional punishments while she is in bed arrest. Perhaps you would like to give her "hourlies". These are spankings given every hour during a set period. She needs to make sure that her master knows it is time for her hourly spanking (or other prescribed hourly punishment) or risk having addition time added to her sentence.

15. Additional general advice to the master. Guys you need to hold strong and be firm. That can be tough. Make sure she takes you seriously throughout this period.

The End

Book #3 - Spanking Romance

By T. Killian

Copyright (C) 2014

Spanking Romance

Chapter One

Hello I'm slave anna. My master is very demanding and strict. He controls my life in almost every way. I pleasure my master many times a week. I'm also available to any of his friends if he wishes.

Master is a firm believer of keeping his slave well disciplined and has a big collection of paddles, slappers, straps, whips, floggers, heavy rulers and more. It's my job to keep them organized and in order. I also have to keep all his toys clean and organized.

Master spanks me on average about twice a day. It's something he genuinely loves to do. Usually master always gives me a spanking before bedtime. That spanking is among my favorite as it helps make me sleepy. If a friend comes over that's into BDSM he'll let him or her spank me also if they want. I don't think he thinks I can be spanked enough. I am not allowed to wear any cloths at home unless we are expecting vanilla company or if it's cold. Master also has a cage in the basement that I get put in, often in preparation for playtime or if he's angry with me. When Master is horny I have to particularly be careful as he'll punish me for the smallest of things.

Master's friend Master Alex came over for a visit yesterday and as usual I was tied up naked on the half table, spanked and taken. The half table is several feet long with stirrups so my legs are kept straight up in the air. My arms and lower pelvis are strapped to the table. My d-cup breasts are also now securely in place should they be the focus of attention, as they often are. On the half table my pussy and asshole are right on the edge of the table so they can be played with and taken with ease. When I'm being spanked on my tits or ass I usually will be required to cum at some point, which is no problem for me. Yesterday while taking me in my pussy Master Alex finally let me cum and wow was that ever a great orgasm.

Typically in the morning I wake up and fix Master breakfast. He may call me into the bedroom to pleasure him if he is in the mood, particularly if it's the weekend. While he's naked, or in his underwear, he'll gives me a good over the knee spanking before he goes to work. He says it helps get his blood pumping and be more ready for the day. Those morning spankings can really wake me up fast. It's usually always with a paddle. Master doesn't usually spank me with his hand anymore, he used to several years ago. As Master is paddling me in the morning, he will tell me what he wants me to do that day, assuming there is something he has on his mind.

I have to admit that today was different as Master started the day very angry with me. I was supposed to go shopping the day before and get more toilet paper but I forgot and didn't go shopping. He found out as he was doing his morning business. He called me into the bedroom, ordered me to crawl from the bedroom door to the foot of the bed and was lecturing me about being forgetful. He hates it when I'm forgetful but unfortunately it's something I have a problem with.

I knew I was in a lot of trouble. I could see he was winding up to really spank me hard. I apologized of course but that rarely does any good. He ordered me to put the chair up in the middle of the bedroom and get the large black wooden paddle. He ordered me to bend over the back of the chair so my hands were on the chair seat, and my butt was the highest thing on me. I looked back at him as he came over, careful not to look at his eyes of course. What I saw made me cringe. He looked really mad. He was scolding me as he ordered me to count out the swats. He started by tapping my butt many times with the big paddle then, to my surprise put the large wooden paddle on the bed nearby and went and got the black leather strap. It was the first spanking implement we ever ordered together. It's falling apart but still packs quite a punch. He started right in on my butt with it. *Slap...slap...slap...SMACK, SMACK, BAM, BAM, SMACK, SMACK...* Sure I'm required to hold still but it's not easy when he gets in a mood like this. I began moaning after the 7th spank or so then gave progressively louder yelps after the 15th. Usually though I can usually take a very hard spanking. My butt's toughen up a bunch over the years.

Master kept scolding me about forgetfulness and laziness. He's had trouble with me about this before. *Smack, smack...smack, BAM, BAM, BAM.* My butt cheeks were bouncing around from the blows and getting redder and redder. Since Master was pressed for time I think he spanked harder and faster. After the 60th or so spank I was begging him to stop. *"Ow master, pleaseee I'mmm soorrry."* I was flinching and moving my outstretched butt which is something that unfortunately made his madder. He grabbed me and held me in place as he really laid it on my ass. I knew it was getting red by then. SMACK, SMACK, BAM, BAM, SMACK, SMACK. Finally he stopped but instead went to get the big black wooden paddle, the one he had ordered me to bring in the first place. "Move away or block even a single blow and you'll spend the next two days in the cage young lady." "Yes Sir". I meekly said holding on to the seat with all my might. BAM, BAM, BAM, BAM. *"ow, ah, pleasseee, no moore master."* BAM, *BAM, SMACK, SMACK, BAM, slap…slap, slap.* "What is my favorite color for your ass young lady?" Master howled. "Red sir," I sheepishly muttered. "I'm now going to check your pussy and god help you if you're not soaking wet". Master's rule was that I had no more than 30 seconds into a spanking to have a wet pussy. This spanking had lasted a lot longer than that already. He must have not woken up completely because he's usually checking me sooner than that. Master is always looking for a reason to punish me and that would be one of them. I felt his fingers enter my pussy and feel their way around inside of me, he teased my clit and I started to cum immediately but I'm a well trained slave and know better than to cum without permission. *"Master, please may I cum, please, please."* Of course he wouldn't let me cum then and his fingers withdrew, soaking wet. Master rubbed my hot red ass for a bit but I knew the only thing that would stop this spanking would be his not wanting to be late for work. That's one of the great things about our morning spankings. Master doesn't have a lot of time to complete them. "Stand up young lady" he ordered and I pushed myself up from the chair rubbing my sore butt. Master caught me rubbing myself. "Hands up behind your back slave." Master then took the heavy wooden ruler in hand and sat on the chair I was just bent over. "Lay over my lap now." I quickly complied, my open palms on the carpet and my toes were also on the carpet. I would have to stay this way or the spanking would never stop. That was the rule. Master rubbed the heavy wooden ruler over my ass. "I love how red your ass gets from a good spanking" he said. "Thank you master." I mumbled. The truth was that by rubbing the ruler over my well spanked ass like that, felt good, but that sensation would abruptly change. BAM!! Wow no warm up but hard spanks right from the gitgo. *BAM, BAM...SMACK, SMACK, BAM, slap...slap, smoosh, slap, bam, BAM.* I was crying now. *"No please Master, I'll be good, I swear."* BAM, SMACK, SMACK, BAM, slap. Tears were willowing up in my eyes . ""Ow master, I'm sorry, I won't dooo it again, I swearr." Now master was spanking me in rapid succession. He really like spanking that way. The side and the top of the right cheek was getting most of the attention for 2 or 3 minutes then it was the left cheek's turn. After 50 or so really hard swats on each cheek, his spanking tempo slowed and his spanking intensity slowed. The end of this spanking was near. "There" Master finally stopped the deluge and looked down at his slave's reddening ass proudly. "A job well done. Get up. You may rub yourself." I stood up and furiously rubbed my butt. This was definitely a harder spanking for a morning spanking than usual; little did I know how much more was to come.

Master sent me to stand in the corner. I still was rubbing my ass but the sniffling had stopped. Master liked to hear me cry in some manner after receiving a good spanking. He came over to me on his way out of the bedroom. He pulled my hands away from my butt and started rubbing my hot red butt cheeks. Suddenly it dawned on me what could happen, I couldn't believe I had just thought of it. "I'm going to ask some folks to come over while I'm gone and have them also punish you. You will serve them also if they want. You will remain naked until I tell you differently." "Yes Master" I gulped.

Master knew many people in the BDSM scene. Several times before Master has had them come over to the house to punish me. I have also had to go to their places, typically in a short skirt and no panties, and get punished at their convenience. Sometimes we have BDSM parties and slaves like me would entertain the masters and mistresses. Those that allowed it would let their slaves be played with by the other dominants and submissives. Typically all the participating slaves would go one at a time to each master and mistress in the room and ask how they can serve them. Usually we would be spanked and have our pussies and tits played with. Some would require that we cum from it. We also would give hand jobs and blowjobs and eat pussy if they wanted it, and of course it would be our responsibility to clean up after they came. There were vibrators and dildos all around and they would be used on us slaves by others as we kneeled in front of our betters. The lucky masters and mistresses though got to do a lot more with us later. I wanted to note that all going to these parties were first required to be tested for STDs.

After a female slave had gone around the room serving the Doms and Dommes, she would be tied down on her back to a padded table, her pussy and anus on its edge, and the masters and mistresses would take turns taking her. All were required to use condoms, including those using strap-ons. I remember one night, while tied down, helpless and vulnerable, my pussy was taken 15 times. 6 masters took me once each, 3 masters took me twice and 3 mistresses used a strap-ons on me. That night my Master was not allowing anyone to take me in my ass, but some nights he would. My pussy would feel so hot afterwards. I suspect it was all the friction. Sometimes I would be sore for days from this. Of course I had to cum for everybody that took me which wasn't as easy later in the night but I didn't want to be punished. I should note that the masters weren't only taking me but also taking the other female slaves so they wouldn't spend as much time in me as they would normally.

Anyway, as Master was leaving for work he said that he would be back for lunch to punish me again and he would also send Master John over in the morning to punish me as well. Clearly this was going to be a long day. Happily Master released me from the corner as he walked out the front door and I now had some time to collect my thoughts.

Chapter Two

My butt heals fast, probably because it's been spanked so much. Its redness goes away surprisingly fast and frankly Master doesn't like that. He'd prefer watching me walk around the house naked with a well spanked, red, marked butt. Bruises show up on my butt but they too go away surprisingly fast. The fact is I would need all those physical characteristics to get through this incredibly spank-filled day.

I put the paddles, straps and other spanking implements away in the closet where they hang or lay in draws. I made our bed and tidied up the room. Master had ordered me to be naked so I didn't have to decide what to wear. I went into the kitchen and cleaned it up. The biggest problem for me was that I was now horny and there was no way I could cum without a Dom or Domme's permission.

I laid down on my bed recalling the already busy morning when the phone ran. I saw it was master' number and quickly answered it. "I am going to take care of your laziness once and for all young lady." Oh oh, this didn't sound good. "Today you will get spanked 9 more times. And I mean good spankings, not love taps. If that doesn't do the trick it will be repeated every week from now on. You know I'll have no problem finding people to spank you and if I have the time that won't even be necessary."

My mouth dropped open. "But Master it will hurt so much." "Good" was his reply. Master John should be there to spank you anytime now." With that he hung up. I was stunned. I tried to think back to the most spankings I've had in a day and if it was a day that included one of those sex parties, I'd say 15 but the spankings I often got at a sex party was short and often not that forceful. Oh my gosh. Suddenly I wasn't horny at all but very concerned, then I heard the doorbell, oh oh, here comes another spanking.

I got out of bed, naked of course, and put my slippers on. I hurried to the door. Looking through the peephole I saw Master John. I let him in, keeping my eyes down of course. "Your owner asked me to come by and give you a good spanking. I hear you were forgetful again." "Yes sir" I muttered, still stunned by my Master's news. "Very well, go fetch my favorite paddle, the brown and gold one." "Yes sir."

The brown and gold paddle was a gift to my master from his father who was also a master. It's about 2 feet long and maybe a third of an inch thick. It has holes in it and a black leather handle. It's nasty but I have a very tough butt.

I got back to the living room and Master John had already gotten out of his cloths. "Crawl to me slave". I quickly got down on all 4s and crawled to him, giving him the paddle. "Kneel in front of me slave, hands on my legs." I gave him the paddle. My mouth was now only a couple of feet from his cock. Unexpectedly I felt a tremendous urge to suck on it. My horniness had returned. "Suck" he ordered. Master John was pretty predictable. I would suck on his cock for a while as he spanked me with the long paddle. Fortunately I am well trained and won't clamp my teeth down on his manhood as he spanked. Also the intensity of his spanking at the moment was not that bad. He was after all being sucked on and didn't want to tempt fate. I do have teeth. I knew from experience that he would soon stop spanking and play with my breasts as I sucked on his cock, invariably ordering me to cum. Oh god I can't wait. I lost track of how many spanks I was getting. I was however ready to cum but knew better than to try to ask. "Faster slave". My head bobbed up and down faster on his cock as I feverishly played with his balls. Master had always taught me to play with a man's balls while I was sucking on his cock. Holding a cane, he would watch me as I sucked on a cock to see if I would dare disobey him in that regard. (As I noted earlier, he is very strict.) If he thought I was not playing hard enough with a man's balls he would say "head up" and I would lift my head off of his cock and he would cane my bottom to everyone's delight.

Then it happened, Master John reached down and commenced playing with my d-cup breasts. He was always good at it and I could wait no longer. I stopped sucking momentarily and begged "please sir may I cum?" He said yes and I nearly saw stars. I had to keep sucking hard though or he'd stop playing with my breasts and immediately start my beating. I shuttered some and hesitated momentarily but caught myself and kept sucking as hard as I could. I thought I did quite an impressive job to be honest. I made gurgling noise as I sucked and came. My tits kept being played with, it was great. After about 10 minutes of heaven I was ordered over his lap as he sat on the couch. Oh that's right, the spanking, that's mainly what he's here for. Well at least I was recharged after that orgasm. Besides my butt was already broken in for the day, how bad could it be?

The other thing I wanted to mention is that Master John was a very sensual master and liked his sub/slave playmates to cum a lot. He is also a gentleman so he started the paddling easy and worked his way up to the hard stuff. "I hear you are being lazy and forgetful again and your owner wants to nip this in the bud." He was spanking now as he spoke. "Yes sir" I managed to say. He was spanking faster and harder now. *BAM, BAM, SMACK, slap, slap, smoosh, slap, bam, BAM.* He was spanking harder than usual and man it hurt. "I had a slave that was lazy and this is just what I gave her. You cannot spank a lazy forgetful slave too much." BAM, SMACK, SMACK, BAM, slap BAM, SMACK, SMACK. "Yes sir" I was now holding back tears and biting on a couch pillow. *"ow, oh, pleassse no morre, oow, oh, ow"* I mumbled. He then spoke "Your master insisted on me spanking you good and hard and that young lady is what I'm going to do." He started spanking real hard and in rapid machine gun-like fashion. That was it. The dam broke and I started crying. *"I won't be lazy sir I prooomise."* I started kicking my legs a little but I knew better than to move my butt away. Darn master John was strong too. Suddenly he stopped. I couldn't believe it. "Give me your right hand". I gave it to him and he pulled it across the small of my back, now he had made me more immobile. "Beg for the spanking to continue." *"Please sir, spank me more."* Like that was an easy thing for me to say. "You can do better than that" he roared. *"Oh please sir paddle my ass until I have learned my lesson and will be a very good girl."* Well I got my wish and the paddling continued. SMACK, BAM, slap, BAM, SMACK, SMACK. "Oww" was that me that just said that. Wow it was. "Legs spread" he ordered and I quickly spread my legs. He spanked in the areas down by the pussy, the areas that were still white, areas that my Master hadn't even gotten to in his haste. Oh gosh, I have another spanking from Master coming up at lunchtime, and this one isn't even over yet. SMACK, BAM, slap, slap, BAM, SMACK, SMACK, slap. My ass cheeks were bouncing back and forth. Then suddenly he ordered me to cum. I went from *"please stop, ow, ow, oh"* to making guttural sounds and not feeling the paddle at all. "I'm cummingggg" I screamed as I rubbed his legs with my pussy as hard as I could, still the spanking went on, slap, BAM, SMACK, SMACK, SMACK, SMACK. He was spanking very evenly from one cheek to the next, upper cheek then lower cheek and some on the upper legs but I continued to cum as ordered; then suddenly the spanking stopped. His hand went down to my pussy and finger fucked me. I arched my back and came even harder for him. I don't know where he found all that energy but his fingers were going in and out of me like a dynamo. Finally he stopped. He then ordered me off his lap to once again suck on his cock. I hesitated at first as my orgasm was still going on even though nothing was touching my pussy or clit. I worked my way down to his cock. "Suck" he ordered and my mouth went back to work.

I rubbed my ass cheeks with one hand and played with his balls with the other. Once again my cheeks were hot and red. I was dying to look at them but knew better than to stop sucking. I was tasting a lot of Master John's ooze and knew what was coming. He came with a shout and filled my mouth with his cum. He held my head in place on his cock. *"Faster slave"* he ordered and forced my head deeper onto his cock. I drank down all his cum. For many minutes I knelt there making sure to drink down all of Master John's cum. Finally he got up and got dressed as we talked. "I hear you're getting 10 spankings today and that could be repeated soon". "Yes sir." "Well maybe I'll stop by again this week to give you another one." "Yes sir;" like I had a choice.

With his clothes back on Master John left and I went to the tall bathroom mirror to look at my red butt. It still stung but I came so hard during the spanking that I'd have to consider that spanking a breeze. I wish master would let me cum more often when he spanked me but my Master is strict, demanding and controlling. He also pays the bills.

Most of the orgasms I got from Master I got when he took me, something he enjoyed doing very much. He would start by taking me in my pussy, which I was required to exercise to keep nice and tight for him. He would then take me in my ass. Mostly he took me in my ass but I came just as hard from being taken in either my pussy or ass.

Often the two of us would lay together naked in bed. Master is very proud of his property. His hands would wander when lying in bed with his slave girl. Sometimes his fingertips caressed, other times his nails scraped as he explored his slave's body. My nipples would get a lot of attention. When master tired of such torment, perhaps he'd tie my hands together. He would then take his time choosing what toys to use on me next. Perhaps earlier I didn't move fast enough or I made too much noise, waking him from his nap. Or maybe he's just in the mood to paddle my butt. My ass is his property to do what he wishes with after all. He would bend me over his knee, flip up my short skirt, (if I've been allowed to wear any clothes,) and run his nails over my already well-spanked ass. His spanking starts slow and gained momentum: slap, slap, slap, SMACK, SMACK, SMACK. Once my ass is a lovely shade of red he'll send me to fetch his crop, floggers and handcuffs. My bound hands are hooked to the ceiling high above my head, so I have to stretch up on my tiptoes. Then he works my body over with his crop and floggers, gentle taps punctuated with hard smacks. When he's done beating me, he lets me down. With my bound hands in front of me I am lead to our bed. He strips and lays down with his cock on the edge of the bed. I am then ordered to pleasure him. He enjoys watching me wiggle into a position that allows me to put my mouth to good use.

With my well-spanked naked ass now sticking up and out, if someone else walks by I will inevitably get taken. Master likes to watch mistress' use the strap-on in me and will invite them over to watch them do just that, often while I am sucking on his cock.

Anyway, so there I was being all dreamy. I had to write some emails so I went and got on the computer and wrote away. Master's one hour lunch break started at noon and it took him 15 minutes to drive over here and another 15 minutes to drive back. I had to have lunch ready soon. He would spank me first, then eat. That way he had cooled off a bit before heading back to work as spanking me can make him work up a sweat. It was always the same. He would sit on the couch where Master John spanked me, and then proceed to redden my butt there. It was 11:30 so I got all the implements he might want and put them on the coffee table in front of where he would spank me OTK. As he'll be in a hurry, it's doubtful he'll tie my hands together, even though he loves doing that before spanking me. As noon approached I made a plate of food for him, had something to eat myself and went and knelt by the couch in anticipation of my next spanking.

I was only there for about 2 minutes when he walked in and immediately sat in front of me on the couch. "Over my lap young lady" he ordered and I crawled over his lap as I had done so many times before. "Your ass is still warm, nice, but it's not particularly red. Let's see if we can change that." Oh I knew he could. "Now which of these shall I use." Master first picked up a black leather slapper but put it down instead opting for a ping pong paddle. He rubbed my butt tenderly with his hands for a while, then with the paddle. "I see that between my spanking earlier and Master John's spanking we're leaving our mark on your lovely ass. Perhaps after this day and night is done, you will have learned your lesson." "Yes master."

Well the rubbing was fun while it lasted but then master started spanking in earnest. *SMACK... BAM, slap, slap...BAM, SMACK...SMACK, BAM...BAM, slap, slap, slap.* I started squirming. "Hold still slave or you'll spend the next 3 days in the cage except to work, serve and be punished." Gee, that didn't sound like fun. I quickly gained my composure and largely stayed put. SMACK, SMACK, slap, slap, BAM, SMACK, SMACK, SMACK, SMACK... BAM, slap. My butt by now was tender enough for me to really feel the swats. *"Ow, ow, no please, ow, aw, aw, stop please, oh."* "Music to my ears young lady" Master said as he started spanking me harder. "Oh please no, ow." I grabbed once again on to the couch cushion and held onto it with all my might. Fortunately my butt began acclimating to the blows and the pain tapered off some. Then master started with the irregular blows. I hate those. He'd rub my butt with the paddle then quickly raise it and bring it down on me, many times in rapid succession. *"Now let's see how fast I can give you 50".* I didn't just hear 50 did I? SMACK, BAM, slap, BAM, slap, slap, BAM, SMACK. I was squirming as the blows really hurt. I tried to stay in place as much as possible. I raised and lowered my butt some from the pain. RAT, TAT, TAT, BAM, BAM, SMACK, BAM. *"Stop pleassssse Master, I'll be gooooodd."* 29, 30, 31, 32, he counted out. I started kicking my feet some but caught myself and held back as much as I could. I cried as he started the 20s. He was now spanking with all his might. *"Ow, no master, stop, oww, ow."*

Abruptly master pushed me off his lap and dropped the paddle. I rubbed my scorching bottom. "Kiss my foot." I crawled over to master and kissed his left shoe. "Lick it slave". I lathered it up with my tongue, then he pulled his foot away and bent over to inspect his work as I held my naked ass up in the air. "Not bad for a quickie. Tonight your tits get it also and it will be an all night affair. I'll give you all the spankings left to make 10 for the day." Master went into the kitchen to eat. I stayed there on my hands and knees. Soon he came out and grabbed his car keys. "You're going to have more visitors this afternoon. You'll take their punishment and serve them." "Who will be punishing me master?" "Master Craig and Master Ted. Master Craig should be here anytime. I need to go. Now go stand in the corner and wait for Master Craig." "Yes master." I stopped rubbing my butt and walked over to the corner putting my nose against where both walls meet. I heard the front door close as master left.

My butt was sore, three good spankings in this short of a period was the real thing. I wanted to go look in the tall bathroom mirror at how red my butt was but my orders were to stay in the corner until Master Craig got there.

Master Craig was a good friend of my Master and they have shared slaves before. I knew what a visit from Master Craig meant, a tit whipping. Master Craig loved to play with and beat tits. I've never seen anyone quite like him when it comes to that. He has a tit fetish I think. On the other hand he sure knows how to make them feel good. I hope that today will be one of those times.

Chapter Three

Sure enough I didn't have to wait long. Master had left the door unlock and soon master Craig walked in. "Hello my dear, your master requested my assistance in punishing you and I was oh so eager to be of service. Aren't you grateful?" "Yes sir" What was I going to say. "I haven't whipped those lovely tits of yours in a while have I?" "No sir." "Frankly I've missed them. I see you're undressed, good."

Master Craig was quite good looking. He's a tennis pro. "Come kneel in front of me young lady." I took my nose away from the corner and walked over to him. He was sitting on the couch where I had recently gotten spanked. "Kneel". I knelt in front of him with my hands behind my head. He caressed and played with my tits. He had always really liked them. "Up high on your knees young lady" he ordered. My breasts were now at his mouth level and he began sucking away on them. I begged to cum but he ignored me, as if he never even heard it. He pulled both nipples into his mouth and sucked on them at the same time. My knees buckled from the pleasure. I don't think it was an orgasm but I continued begging for permission to cum, no such luck.

Master Craig then released my tits and pulled me towards him by the back of my head for a kiss. He had done this before but I had forgotten about it. He then had me remove his clothing. He then leaned back on the couch and ordered me to suck on his cock.

I had been taught that when I suck on a cock, I am to stick my butt up and out so it can be enjoyed and otherwise used by others. By using long implements my ass can now also be beaten by the person I'm pleasuring. I hadn't seen it when I had originally come over but next to him, Master Craig had put his long red flogger. "Suck harder slave" I heard him say as he rested the flogger on my back. I sucked hard. At least I'm not going to get spanked hard if I'm sucking on his cock.

Master Craig really took care of himself. He ate well, worked out, didn't smoke, etc and I could tell by how good his ooze tasted. I love good tasting ooze and I lapped it up eagerly. Suddenly he began flogging my upturned butt. *FLOP, FLACK, SMACK, CRACK...CRACK, BAM...FLOP, SMACK.* The flogger kept landing mostly on my butt but he also flogged my back. He wasn't beating me particularly hard, besides I didn't care because I loved sucking on his cock and the beating was just getting me hornier.

Suddenly it stopped. "Head up young lady." I forced myself to stop sucking and took my head away from that lovely cock. I kept my eyes on it hoping that being away from it would be just a temporary thing, but it was not to be. "Your Master tells me your forgetfulness has returned and he wants it to end.' "Yes sir." "Clearly then you need quite a bit of discipline for such a thing. We're going to start with a spanking and then a tit whipping. You know how I love to whip those gorgeous tits of yours." "Yes sir." "Give me your hands." I clapped my hands together on his lap and he tied them securely together. He then motioned me to lay over his lap which I did. He began rubbing my already tender butt. "Legs spread". I spread my legs about 2 feet wide. He then stuck 2 fingers up my pussy. Wow did they ever easily slide in. "Wow, you are one wet little slave girl. Very good. But no you're not cumming yet."

Master Craig started my spanking with his hand. He went right to work too, *SMACK, SMACK, BAM, BAM, slap, slap, BAM, SMACK, SMACK, BAM, slap.* I lost count as to how many spanks. I had also forgotten how much Master Craig liked to spank with his hand. Now he was spanking hard, smiling down on me as I squirmed and moaned. "I don't accept forgetfulness in a slave so why should your owner? "I understand sir" was all I could muster. *BAM, BAM, CRACK, CRACK, slap, slap, BAM, SMACK, SMACK.* My ass was already tender from the day's abuse so I was feeling this more than usual. I kicked my legs some. Master Craig was really laying it on fast and furious. Then suddenly I found myself on the verge of cumming. I knew Master Craig wouldn't let me cum so why ask. I continued to yelp, moan and squirm. I thought I might cry when suddenly I started cumming, even though I didn't mean to. I tried hard not to move my pelvis in a manner that would give away that I was cumming without permission but suddenly Master Craig's scolding and spanks meant a lot less. Then Master Craig stopped using his hand, reached for a strap and continued the deluge on my ass, rubbing it periodically to admire his work. I had a nice controlled orgasm as he scolded and spanked me. *SMACK, BAM...BAM, slap, slap, BAM, SMACK..SMACK, SMACK, slap.* I turned back to look at my ass and it was red. "Eyes forward" he scowled giving me 5 really hard strokes to punctuate it. The spanking now was really hurting and as I had lost concentration, I also lost my orgasm, now all I felt was pain. *"Ow, noo sir, stop, oow, ow."* I pounded the couch in pain. He had never spanked me so hard. "Hold your ass still slave." I hadn't realized it but I had lifted my butt up some to avoid the spanks. Wow, that was a bad idea. He went back to work on my ass and upper legs, this time with a medium size rubber paddle. *"Ow, ooh, ooh, pleassee sir, I'llll be good."* Dozens of spanks later I was crying hard. I can take a really hard spanking but all this attention to my ass was really getting to me. Then suddenly it stopped.

"Kneel" was the order and I eagerly knelt in front of him as I rubbed my butt cheeks. "I see we have some tears here" he said looking into my eyes. "Good. I believe the message is getting through to you." "Yes sir" I moaned while rubbing my naked, sore bottom. "Now it's time to give those lovely tits of yours the same kind of attention." Oh great, but at least my butt would get a rest for a change.

I had been trained to easily cum from breast stimulation. I am so proud of my breasts. They give me and others so much pleasure. They can take quite a beating too. Master Craig specialized in tit torture so I suspected my tits would be red soon.

As I knelt in front of him, Master Craig untied my wrists and ordered me to turn around and put my wrists behind my back. He tied my hands behind my back. He then reached over my shoulders and tied my boobs fairly tightly together at their base. My tits were even firmer than usual now. Their nipples quickly hardened. He pinched both nipples hard waking me from my dreamy state and making me yelp. "What is my favorite color for your tits slave?" "Red sir." "You're darn right, especially if you're being punished. What do your tits exist for?" "To be played with and beaten sir." "Good girl."

Master Craig then took out a short tit flogger and proceeded to lightly whip my tits with it as I continued to kneel in front of him. I closed my eyes instinctively but the flogger never came anywhere close to my face. Master Craig really knew how to whip tits. I could tell this was something he really enjoyed doing. He started playing with one of my nipples as he was whipping the other one. This flogging went on for about 15 minutes. He then put the flogger down and took up the same slapper he had earlier used on my butt. He pulled my head back by the hair exposing my breasts more and proceeded to spank them for real. *Slap, slap, SMACK, SMACK, BAM, slap, slap.* Master Craig concentrated spanking the fleshing mounds of the left breast, reaching out, grabbing it by the nipple, pulling it up and separating it from the right breast so more off my large breast was free to spank. It did sting but also felt sinfully good. "A forgetful, lazy slave girl needs to be a well beaten slave girl. Isn't that right young lady*?"* *"Yess sir."* I managed to say. *Smack...slap, slap, slap, SMACK, SMACK, BAM, slap.* He pinched my left nipple as he held it making me wince, but then he twisted it in-between his fingers giving me pleasure. He probably didn't even realize he was playing with the nipple in such a pleasurable way. Giving breasts pleasure and pain is just his nature. I sure wasn't going to complain. Then he let go of my left nipple and got a hold of the right nipple, pulling the right breast out to the right, separating it from its twin, allowing more of it to be beaten. *Slap, slap, slap, SMACK, SMACK, BAM, slap.* "Do you know how much I enjoy beating your tits young lady?" *"Ow, oh...a lot sir."* "Girl do I ever." *Slap, slap, slap, SMACK, SMACK, BAM, slap, slap.* Blow after blow continued to rain down on my breasts, making them pink and tender. He pulled up my right breast by the nipple and concentrated his beating on the underside. It did hurt but frankly I got more pleasure from a tit whipping from him than when he spanks my ass. I glanced down at my breasts and they were getting red. Suddenly I blurted it out "please sir may I cum?" The whipping stopped suddenly as Master Craig looked at me somewhat puzzled. "Wow, you are an amazing slave and I love how masochistic you are." Then he got very serious and got close to me and said "but you know slave that you may not cum. You are being punished and you should know better than to even hope for it." He them grabbed both of my large nipples together with one hand and pulled my breasts up exposing their soft underbelly, going to work on them both at once with the slapper and spanking them hard now. *"Ow, ohh no sir, ow, oww, oh pleeaaseee."* Slap...slap, slap...slap, slap, SMACK, BAM...slap, slap. He let go of my tits and they flopped down. He then proceeded to spank their upper front. "You know how much I love spanking your tits" *"yes sir, ow, ow, oh, ow."* This was really hurting now and I wasn't going to be allowed to cum so I was going to just have to take it.

My breasts were now a shade of red and Master Craig stopped. I thought my tit whipping was over but I was wrong. "Turn around slave." I turned around obediently and knelt there as he untied my wrists. Then in my stupor I remembered that there was another position for me and my tits to be whipped in…and more.

Master Craig led me over to the half table. I was ordered to lay on my back on it. It was a familiar position for me. My pussy and ass were on the table's edge and thus would be easy to play with and take. My back and head were lying on the table. The ankles and thighs got tied to the stirrups. A strap came over my lower pelvis to keep it in place and straps held each arm in place. I was now quite vulnerable and immobile.

My master put me here often and left me here for his and other's pleasure. My legs are positioned such that my butt can be easily spanked and I could be taken both in my pussy and ass. But for the time being Master Craig was a lot more interested in finishing the job he started with my tits. Now though he would use the big black flogger to beat them. This part would make me cry but leave my pussy dripping.

Master Craig bent down to my pussy and sucked the copious amount of cum out of it. "You know what's coming now young lady don't you." "Yes sir" I think I said. He raised the flogger and CRACK. "Ow". CRACK, CRACK..SMACK. This is a big room so he could raise up the big flogger and let it fly. *CRACK, CRACK..SMACK, BAM...SMACK, BAM.* I was now crying and trying to move away but to no avail. I was held too tightly in place and could go nowhere. BAM, SMACK, BAM. He was working up a sweat and loving every second of it. "Are you still going to be a forgetful slave?" "No sir". I was so exposed and I knew by now my pussy was dripping wet. I couldn't wait for him to take me like he always did. And he would take me for a long time too. I held onto that thought as the blows rained down on my chest. *"Please sir, oww, oww, ahhh."* Master Craig was very skilled and the flogger never landed more than a couple of inches above my breasts. Finally it was over but I kept whimpering.

He now played with my sensitive breasts grabbing, kneading, twisting, turning and holding them. "I am so proud of my work. Your breasts are so much fun to work with. You know your tits are my favorite tits to whip." Oh lucky me. "Thank you sir." I whimpered. He bent down and lightly bite my nipples one by one, also sucking on them and playing with my breasts more. He was so proud of his work and really did love my tits. Suddenly I remembered what was to come next, yes this would be great.

I looked down at my chest and it was red. My nipples were hot and sensitive. I heard Master Craig doing something and I looked over at him. His cock was hard and he was coming over to my exposed holes. First he got out some lubricant and used it and his finger to lubricate my anus. He inserted his finger deep into my ass making me moan in anticipation. He then cleaned off his finger with a paper towel. "Beg for it slave" he ordered. *"Sir please take me with your big, hard cock"*. "You can do better than that." *"Please sir I'm begging, please take me with your big hard cock and fuck me hard because I've been such a bad slave. I need to be fucked hard to clear my head and not be forgetful."* Satisfied he then entered my pussy. Immediately I began begging to cum, which he allowed me to do.

Master Craig grabbed my upper legs to hold me in place while he pounded my pussy with his cock. I came so hard. I lost track of what time it was. "Come harder slut" he roared and I did just that, pumping my hips against him as he took me. I couldn't wait for him to take me in my ass. "You like how this feels in that naughty little cunt of yours don't you slave." "Yes sir" I stammered. He pounded me harder and buried his cock all the way into my pussy, just leaving it there for a few moments as he gyrated his hips, making it move from side to side. I was so wet that it slide easily in my pussy. "Wow, you're one soaking wet little slave girl." I couldn't answer though I think I tried, I was cumming too hard. A little while later he pulled out of my pussy and stuck his cock in my ass. *"Ohhhhh sir, yes, thank you....ohhh."* He started taking me slowly in the ass at first but built up speed and after a couple of minutes was pounding my butthole with vigor. I felt pain, and waves of ecstasy.

Master Craig finished taking me a while later. He left me there tied down, exhausted and helpless. My tits were a shade of red and my ass sore and tender. "I hope you will learn your lesson today young lady but then again I hope you don't as I do love these sessions so much. Your owner said to leave you like this as Master Ted will be here soon to do as he wishes with you. What have you to say?" *"Thank you sir for disciplining and taking me."* "Good girl." With that he left.

Chapter Four

There I was alone and tied down waiting for the next person to punish and ravage me. It wasn't that big of a deal as I've been on this table like this often. I sure hope I don't have to go to the bathroom while no one is here though. Fortunately it's usually not a problem. Master always talked about putting a mirror on the wall across from my upturn legs, ass and pussy. That would be nice as I could see how red my ass was. Strapped down like this I could only move myself a bit from the tits up as my arms were strapped down which limited my movement.

Master Ted really liked to fuck me in the ass. I don't think he had ever taken me in my pussy. A drawback to Doms in regard to the position I was strapped down to this table in, is that it is difficult for me to suck on their cocks. Mistresses can get on the table and sit on my face for me to pleasure them. Master Ted has had me in this position before so I was expecting the usual ass whipping and ass fucking. I didn't really like Master Ted that much and I don't think he's a particularly good lover but I had no say in the matter.

Then I heard someone enter, man I hope that's Master Ted, and I could tell from his voice that it was. "Wow, look at you. All ready to be beaten and taken." I wasn't sure if I was supposed to answer so I didn't say anything. I heard him undressing. "I'm going to fuck you silly bitch. I heard about your forgetfulness and laziness, well I'm here to beat it right out of you." I heard noises like he was getting something together to spank me with. "Any requests for what I should spank you with?" "Your hand sir?" "Nice try but you know how I like the belt." No not the belt. He had a wide leather belt that he had had for ages. The rustling I heard must have been him taking it off his pants. He likes to wear it around when he's going to whip a slave with it. He looked over and felt my ass. "How many spankings have you gotten today young lady?" "Four so far sir." "Wow, your ass looks surprisingly good for all that, you always could take quite a spanking." "Thank you sir." He then came over and began playing with my tits, each hand on a tit. "Man I love these tits, especially when they have such a nice red hue like now. What do you say slave?" "Thank you sir." Getting my tits played with again felt good. They were still smarting from the tit whipping though but gratefully were gifting me with some pleasure. I started to groan seductively and move my head slowly back and forth. I knew he wouldn't let me cum so I didn't even try asking.

"Guess what I'm going to beat your ass with?" "Your belt sir?" "Good girl, you remember well." I heard some rustling then I felt him lubing up my anus for after the beating. Then suddenly I felt nothing. That's trouble. Past my upturn legs and exposed pussy I heard him whipping the air with the belt. Oh man, this is not good. Then he lightly swung the belt against my ass many times. It was just the start of things to come. It would be my worst beating of the day so far. *SMACK, BAM, BAM...SMACK, SMACK, SMACK, BAM.* I yelled out from the beginning, making his cock hard no doubt. He grabbed my legs and drew himself closer to me. The whipping continued. SMACK, SMACK, SMACK, BAM, BAM, BAM, BAM. I tried to move my ass but it was too securely in place. Then I realized I was crying *"Ow, ow, no please, ow, aw, aw, stop please, ohhh, nnnno."* He pulled my ass out as far as the pelvic strap would allow, all in an effort to expose as much ass as possible. SMACK, SMACK, SMACK, BAM, BAM. Master Ted was in heaven, he is a sadistic Dom with cart blanche to punish a wayward slave girl. I could not escape the blows that were raining down on my ass. *"I'mmm begging masterr, pleaseee."* BAM, SLAP, Slap, BAM...SMACK. Tears were running down my cheeks. I can usually take a good beating but as sensitive as my ass was from the days' previous onslaught and this brute of a master wailing away on my tender ass with a big belt, was too much. I don't think my master would even be happy about this. I know this would leave plenty of marks on my ass. *"Masterrrr, pleaaaasse, oh, aw, pleassse stoppp pleaaaase, oh."*

Something on my ass felt different then I realized that the beating had stopped. Master Ted had also whipped my upper legs, something my owner will not like. Leaving marks on my legs, or on anyone else's property, is not good etiquette. I continued to cry. I didn't hear back from him but I heard him making himself harder and I knew the beating was over. He would concentrate now on my relaxed asshole. I felt him come up to me, grab both my hips and thrust himself into me..... *"ohhhh"* I shuttered glad to be feeling another type of sensation but my ass was still on fire.

Master Ted always grunted a lot when he fucked. It sounded real animal-like but a cock in my ass was a welcome change and soon I felt an orgasm coming on. Oh god, I hope this meany will let me cum. *"Permission to cum sir please."* No answer. *"Please sir may I cum....oh please, please."* I hate him. I tried hard to not cum and I was able to stifle the orgasm.

Doms like him give BDSM a bad name as far as I was concerned. I don't get taken by him often and was going to talk to master about him, still his cock pounding my ass did feel good, even if I couldn't cum. I laid back and enjoyed it. At least 5 of my beatings for the day were over-with.

Chapter Five

I lay there on my back with my legs in the stirrups, exhausted. I remained strapped down to the table. I began reminiscing about the 5 hard spankings I'd had so far today. I knew I had 5 more to go, and as my ass and tits were quite tender and sore, I suspected those would be tough. I didn't know who else Master had invited to come punish me at this point but his good friend Master Alex was certainly one.

I had been strapped down to this table for two long hard spankings, one of which included a tit whipping. Unfortunately nobody counts the tit whipping as a separate spanking which wasn't fair in my opinion. Master Ted, the last person to punish and take me while strapped down, had left me here, as did Master Craig before him. I didn't mind being strapped down to the table terribly because it was comfortable and I had become tired from all the day's attention. So I dozed off to get some well deserved rest.

I was awakened a while later as much to my surprise, my very own wonderful master walked in. He explained that he brought the rest of his day's work home. He told me that he had been keeping up on my day's activity, then came over, inspected me and ran his hands over my lightly reddened breasts. "Wow, I bet your tits and ass are nice and tender by now." He inspected me further. "Before I get back to work though and while you're so conveniently strapped down, I young lady will now give you spanking #6."

Master went into the kitchen and got something to drink. From there he went into his bedroom and took off his clothes. Even though master is so strict and controlling, I must admit that I do love him and love serving him. He really does have my best interests in mind. I also love to see my master naked and it almost instantly turns me on. Master's ooze is so tasty and I frankly can't suck on his cock enough. If anything, master doesn't let me suck on his cock as much as I'd like. Hopefully I would have another opportunity real soon.

I didn't know what he had in mind for me. A lot depended on how horny he was. I already had a tit whipping, which was evident by my pink chest, so I didn't think he would give me that, at least until tonight. My guess was that with my strapped legs still in the air and my ass so easily accessible on the edge of the table, I would have at least the first part of spanking #6 here.

Master came over. "Eyes closed slave." I quickly shut my eyes but was saddened to have to lose sight of master.

Master had put on some kind of gloves. I just barely got a glimpse of them before being ordered to close my eyes. Somehow they looked different.

I could tell master was next to my tits now. Oh no, it's the gloves with the hundreds of tiny nubs on them. Then master ran the large black and gray nubbed gloves over my tender tits. *"Oh...oh master"*. Well it hurt actually but as I'm a sexual masochist, any attention, positive or negative, that my tits get, tends to be enjoyable. Then master squeezed both breasts hard with his gloved hands. That sure got my attention. My back arched and by reflex I thrust my pelvis up. Master kept up the pressure and now was kneading my nipples with the nubbed gloves. "No pleassee master." Then he began spanking my tits with his nub gloved hands. Well looks like master was going to beat my tits now after all. *"Ow..ohhh..owww."* Master picked up the tempo and intensity of the tit spanking. *Slap..slap, Bam, slap, smack..slap, bam, bam, bam, slap.* Master grabbed my left tit by the nipple and lifted it straight up in the air, exposing more breast flesh that way. Of course now there was more for him to spank. BAM, SLAP, smack..slap, slap, bam, bam, SMACK. I bit my tongue some. It was a strange pain and frankly wasn't turning me on...that much. Master pulling on my nipple with the nubbed gloves particular hurt. The tit spanking continued...*BAM, slap, SMACK...slap, BAM.* Master released the nipple he was holding up to spank around and went back to vigorously rubbing and kneading both my tits with the nubbed gloves. It was painful but there was some pleasure mixed in there. *"Mmmm...ohhhhh...master."* "You can't fool me, I know you, you're about ready to cum from this." Master said. Then he gave each tit 5 quick swats and that was it.

I took a deep breath as Master took the gloves off and put them on a table nearby. The bad news is he picked up a paddle and was heading my ass' way. "What have we learned about being forgetful in my house young lady? Master said to me sternly. "That you won't tolerate it master." "Exactly."

Master was standing beside my ass now and massaging it roughly, he then pinched my redden globes many times. "Ow" I instinctively said. Master put a finger in my pussy to make sure I was wet. With the attention I just had, even though it was painful, I was still required to get wet. I did not let him down. Then much to my surprise master bent down and sucked on my wet pussy, I immediately begged to cum. *"Master pleassse may I...ohh may I cum?"* No answer, but there was no way I could stop from cumming if master is going to keep eating me for any length of time. *"Oh God please Master pleassse may I cummm?"* Thankfully he stopped. I exhaled then remembered master was still angry with me and standing next to my butt with a paddle. I guess you know what happened next. SMACK, SMACK, SMACK, SMACK, SMACK. *"Oh, ow, ohhhh, oh, master, oww."* Master really laid it on my butt, swinging hard and fast, SMACK, BAM, SMACK, SMACK, BAM, SLAP, SLAP, BAM. I was so strapped down that I couldn't move and had to just lay there with my already well spanked butt sticking out to take master' punishment. SMACK, SMACK, SLAP, SLAP, SMACK, BAM. Thank goodness master wasn't making me count the licks because he was spanking too fast and it really hurt now. I pulled on my arm restraints but it was no use. I was now crying. *"Owww, I'lll be ggood, owwwwwww, please master."* "What are you not going to do young lady" master bellowed, breathing hard from spanking with so much vigor. "Be forgetful sir." Suddenly the spanking stopped. I probably got 80 stokes but since they were so fast I actually wasn't being spanked for that long. I don't think they were his hardest strokes either. Whatever the case was, once again my ass was on fire and I could do nothing about it. Master again bent down and sucked on my pussy, getting all the new pussy juice I created from the spanking. Man that felt good. It almost made me stop feeling my raw butt, not quite though. All the spankings I would get now really would hurt with my ass being so tender.

I heard master doing something. I was concentrating so much on my scalding ass that I didn't see master getting ready to take me. But then I saw it and suddenly my butt didn't feel as bad. Usually master would take me for 20-30 minutes and man was I ever ready for it. Master entered my pussy and immediately ordered me to cum. It slide effortlessly in. He then started to fuck his slave to his heart's content. He started slowly then started to really pound me.

Master's breathing got heavier and his grunting got more intense. *"Cum harder slave"* he ordered and I happily obeyed. I loved it when I helped make my master feel good like that and the events of the day I think are really turning him on. Master and his slave would soon feel quite sexually satisfied. Unfortunately for me, I knew that wasn't the last time master was going to beat me today. I did after all have 4 more spankings to go.

Chapter Six

Master took me for around 30 glorious minutes. About 15 minutes into taking me in my pussy, he suddenly remembered my ass and entered my asshole, taking me there for the rest of the time. Either hole made me cum just as hard so it didn't matter where he took me as far as I was concerned. Master finished exhausted. He re-gained his composure and unstrapped me from the table. Good thing because I had to go to the bathroom. Master took a shower and thankfully had no orders for me so I got some lunch and went into our bedroom. It was almost 2:30 now. I tried sitting down on my desk chair to check my email but my butt wasn't ready for that so I put a special inflatable pillow in the shape of a ring on the seat I have used before for such occasions. Fortunately that helped. Man it's a good thing I had such a tough butt. With email checked I went and laid down on my stomach but now I felt my tender tits. I turned over and lay on my back. That worked okay as long as I kept my legs up and most of the weight on my back.

Meanwhile Master had gone into his study and was working on something he really needed to concentrate on. I didn't turn on the bedroom TV on or make any noise. Maybe he'd forgotten that I was there because usually in these situations, he'd put me in one of the cages in the basement.

Master had two cages custom built for me. They were in the basement. The basement is a finished basement except for the big separate room that has the cages and play equipment. That room had a dungeon like appearance. Its floor was covered in linoleum that had a stone like appearance. The walls were made of cement which had a number of hooks and racks preset into the cement as it was originally poured. Also in there are a wooden X type table and a number of different types of wooden horses for us slaves to be bent over and tied down to. I guess you can imagine what happens after that.

One of the cages could hold more than one slave. It was my favorite. It had a comfortable, padded floor and a convenient opening big enough for me to bend over and stick my ass through to the outside for folks to do whatever they wanted with. With my ass sticking out of the cage in the manner I just mentioned, master would reach his hand into the cage and put a strap around my front pubic area to securely hold my butt out of the cage and in place. He would then beat my ass to his heart's content. Of course I could also be taken in that position.

I was awoken from my dream state by master calling for me and ordering me into his office. I entered and knelt down in front of him with my eyes down and my hands clasped behind my neck. He fondled my breasts for a while, looked at me and said. "It's important that you understand that I am doing this for your own good. You need this discipline to make you a more complete person. I have your best interests in mind." He caressed my face and hair and pulled me to his lips for a passionate kiss. Oh my god. That made me feel so good. "Thank you master. I know how much you care about me." He gave me a smile and went back to work as I continued to kneel naked in front of him. "You may put your hands down" he said with kindness in his voice.

I would kneel there for about 10 minutes more then he put his pen down said it was time for my seventh spanking and this one he would give me while I was bent over and strapped to the black wooden spanking horse in the basement. He ordered me to go down to the basement and prepare it for my punishment. I said "yes master" and went down to the basement, naked as the day I was born.

The black wooden spanking horse was a great piece of equipment to spank a slave on. The slave's legs are spread to the sides of the horse and securely strapped to each side. The slave's ass is the highest point of her and her pussy and anus are readily available for use. An adaptation that master had made was that instead of the upper torso laying at the same angle *over* the other side of the horse, (thus the head would be bent over the horse and nearing the ground,) the upper body rested on a padded wood support that was parallel to the ground. At roughly the middle of the back was a strap to hold the upper body in place. Wrist straps held both arms in place at the wrist. There was a relatively wide hole for the slave's boobs to hang down through, thus making them readily available to play with or spank. With this set-up, the slave's tits and mouth were readily available for use. Another advantage to this adapted wooden horse set up, from the slave's standpoint, was that her butt cheeks weren't pulled so tight from the body being almost completely bent over. Maybe tighter butt cheeks hurt more from being spanked, I didn't know for sure but thought so.

I could strap my legs down myself to save time, but master would have to strap my upper torso down, as well as both of my wrists. I will largely be immobile and completely vulnerable, just how I like it!

I heard Master come down the steps. I quickly turned my eyes away and looked down at the floor. "Good girl, you're ready to be fully strapped in." Master then strapped my torso down tightly with one strap and then strapped both my wrists down with the other two straps.

Master had brought down his laptop computer to continue working in-between spankings. He went back to work on it for 10 or so minutes, then he went to the closet with the implements and took out a big flogger. I love to get my ass flogged. The floggers are my favorite thing to be beaten with. Maybe master didn't know that, though I had told him before. Maybe master was feeling a little bad about the extreme punishment I was enduring. Of course my ass was really sore already so this flogging would hurt after all. Then...FLOP, and the flogging of my ass started. *FLOP, CRACK, FLOP, BAM, CRACK, BAM, FLOP.* Master really got into it. I made some grunts but the truth was that the kind of pain this flogging *was* giving me, (and it was painful,) was okay. Still I'd better be careful and not need to cum or master will know it's not having the desired effect on me. Fine, I'll make like I'm hurting, then "OWWW!!!"

That's the problem with being flogged with your legs wide open like that, the pussy can take a direct hit, and just did. "Aw, did your pussy get hit. Here, I'll kiss it and make it feel all better." Master then bent down and sucked on my pussy. Wow, that made it feel better okay and immediately I needed to cum. "Please master may I cum?" "No." Master kept sucking on my pussy for about 30 seconds more, making me quiver. Then he reached down with his hand to tap on it instead, like he was thinking about spanking it. Gee I sure hope not, my pussy had escaped the spankings so far. It had been taken quite a bit today and frankly was a bit sore already. But master instead continued the flogging. *CRACK, FLOP, BAM, CRACK, BAM, FLOP.* I pulled on my wrist straps, like that was going to do me any good. *CRACK, BAM, FLOP*. The blows came down loudly and with a regular tempo, not hurting a lot but definitely getting my attention. I suspect master was starting to work up a sweat, something he would rather not do as he already showered once today. Master then put down the flogger and rubbed my butt. He bent down to suck up any more pussy juice I had made for him. He then went back to the closet to get another implement. "Oh yes, the crop. I haven't used that on your ass in at least a week." I looked over at him as he walked back to me swooshing the crop in the air. He positioned himself off to the right of my ass...then...*CRACK, CRACK, CRACK*. "I haven't forgotten why you're here young lady and will make sure your laziness is beaten out of you." "*Oww, ohh*" The crop was landing on my upturned right cheek now in rapid succession, really hard too. I began crying. I clenched my cheeks but that did no good. "I know that a well beaten slave is an attentive slave and you WILL be an attentive slave." At least 25 quick swats landed on my cheeks before he went to my left side and started the whipping again, this time concentrating on my left cheek. CRACK, CRACK, CRACK, BAM, BAM, SMACK, SMACK. I knew how wet my pussy had gotten and I could have cum if ordered to but I knew master was in no mood to let me cum. BAM, SMACK, CRACK, BAM, CRACK. The blows were now landing randomly all over my ass. Master started concentrating his blows on my upper legs. My thighs reddened faster than my ass for some reason and master liked that. Master then stopped long enough to suck up any new pussy juice I had made for him, the whipping then continued. "Count out the last 20 slave" he ordered. CRACK, *"onee"*, SMACK *"two master"*, BAM *"oh..three master"*, CRACK, *"oh, pleaseee, four master."* I counted out all 20 of the licks as ordered and just like that my spanking was done. Master rubbed my hot, sore ass. "We both know how tough it is to get marks to stick on your ass and I am so happy to see your ass so marked up. For days you young lady will be reminded every time you sit down of the importance of not being forgetful." "Yes master." I managed to say. My ass really hurt and I had been crying. Wow would I ever shed a lot of tears before this day was over. "I'm getting the camera. I want to capture this. He kept rubbing my ass. "And to think there are 3 more spankings to go" he said happily.

The digital camera was on the shelf by his table. He got it and snapped a number of photos. He then went and continued to work on his laptop. I stopped crying but softly moaned, wiggling from the pain as I continued to lay strapped down to the horse wishing so much that I could rub myself.

Chapter Seven

I continued to lay over the horse helpless and vulnerable, waiting to be further used and abused. I looked over at Master, waiting for a moment, then when I thought he wasn't concentrating on something, I spoke. "Master" I meekly blurted out. "Yes young lady" he said not looking up from his computer. "Would 10 spankings in one day be the most you ever have given to a slave in your life?" He didn't need to think and quickly answered "Yes." "Well it sure will be a personal best for me." We both had an uncomfortable laugh. There was a pause. "I've had too many problems over the years from your forgetfulness and you know that. This is just the first day like this should that continue to be a problem." I swallowed hard. Oh man that didn't sound good. I mean I've cum a lot today but my ass was really hurting and I had 3 spankings left.

Master then got up, came over and turned the horse I was strapped down to so that my ass, pussy and anus were directly facing him while he worked. I must have made a great sight. He could also see my breasts dangling towards the ground.

I wiggled a bit to adjust myself in the straps. About 15 minutes later, abruptly master came over, bent down and sucked on my pussy. Wow. With each hand he grabbed an asscheek and squeezed hard. I let out a yelp. "Cum for me slave" he yelled and man did I ever. "Ohhhhhh." With each hand he started lightly spanking each cheek, sucking like crazy. This day really must have turned master on as I don't get eaten by him a real lot but he was looking for as much pussy juice as possible and clearly did not think I was giving him enough. "Is that all the pussy juice you're going to give me? Fine, I think we can change that." Man that didn't sound good. He went and got a black leather slapper and started once again sucking but this time while pounding my ass with the slapper. *"Oh owww. I'lll cummm haaarder."* Master then dug his fingernails into my bruised ass cheeks. That made me scream. *"AWWWW"*. He sucked so hard that it hurt but I came as hard as I could and know I gave him a mouthful because the spanking stopped and the eating continued. Several minutes later master left contented and went back to his computer.

"Master" I asked, "does that count as one spanking?" "No such luck dear." Well it was worth a try. All the spankings now were really going to hurt and I knew it. Then the phone rang. Master answered it, it was Master Alex. "Yes she's had seven of them so far and she's tied down ass up on the black horse waiting for you." They talked for a bit and then he hung up. Looking at me he said "Master Alex is driving and almost here. *Good news spanking number 8 is minutes away.*" Good news for who? I squirmed and felt a shiver go down my spine.

Master Alex was a large man who like Master Craig, loved my breasts. He has played with me before while I was in this position. No doubt he would sit in front of me and play with my tits for a while. Like Master Craig he loved my breasts. Everybody loved my breasts. Many minutes past and my owner got up and went upstairs to let Master Alex in. Still more minutes went by. I felt a bit of a chill on my sore ass. I hoped I wouldn't cry from my next spankings but I figured I would. My last one or two spankings of the day would be by master and I figured he would let me have it good. He just loves giving me a good spanking.

I heard the two of them come down and Master Alex immediately commented on my marked red ass. "Wow, this ass looks great. Man, I can't wait to add to that." I shook for a moment with anticipation. Master Alex took off his shirt and pants and revealed a tattooed chest. He now was wearing only his black underwear. It was a very hot look actually. He came over to me while making small talk with my owner and started caressing my beaten ass and upper thighs. It felt good. "I hope you young lady have been learning your lesson." "Yes sir. I have learned my lesson." Both masters had a short laugh from that remark. Then Master Alex took his underwear off. Now everybody in the room was naked, only I was the only one tied down and helpless.

As I predicted, Master Alex sat down in front of me and started playing with my breasts. My breasts, though still sore, were not near as sore as my ass. His hands really felt good though. He then took out a bottle of lotion, put a big glob on each hand and commenced to massage my breasts using the lubrication of the non-desensitizing lotion. That always felt good. (My owner does that to my tits sometimes also.) Within 60 seconds I was ready to cum. I asked for permission and got it. My master then went back to my pussy and started eating me again. Oh my God did I ever cum. I know I gave him lots of pussy juice. With his fingers, Master Alex ran circles around the lubricated fleshy part of my breasts for many minutes making me beg to have my nipples played with. *"Master Alex please play with my nipples so I can give my owner more pussy juice."* That was the way to ask as he suddenly did and my body shook from the intensity of the orgasm. "Awwwwwww yessssss, awwwwwww." Waves of pleasure rolled over me and I strained at my bonds as the spasms engulfed me. *"Awwwwwww."* 10 minutes of this came and went, still master was eating me, then he stopped eating me and went back to his seat. The breast massage would also end a few minutes later. What a divine interlude it was.

Master Alex cleaned off the lotion from my breasts and his hands. He then got closer to me and pushed his cock into my mouth. I sucked for all I was worth. The longer I sucked after all, the longer before my next my spanking would start. After 10 or so minutes of that he went to his bag and pulled out a wooden paddle. Looks like the business of the day was at hand.

"So your forgetfulness has returned young lady?" "Yes sir" I reluctantly admitted. "Definitely that needs to be addressed immediately." With that he went behind me and rubbed the paddle over my butt, then WHACK. I jumped, oh that hurt. WHACK, WHACK, WHACK. "Ow, owww, pleaseee noo." WHACK, WHACK, WHACK. I strained at my bonds and my torso jumped up sending my breasts bouncing up. I started crying after only 5 swats. SMACK, BAM, WHACK, WHACK. *"Nooo..I..won't forgettt."* BAM, WHACK, WHACK, slap, slap. The paddling went on for what seemed very long and my crying really delighted them. *"Oh, please sir, no pleassee."* Tears were now running down my cheeks as the pain was intense. Master Alex was spanking my thighs now, including the middle thighs that had earlier been left unscathed. Back to my ass he went pounding away without mercy. *"Oh god, nooo please..."* I begged. Then my owner intervened. He wanted more of his slave's pussy juice. All I knew was that the spanking had stopped and master was coming over. Once again he bent down and sucked on my pussy looking for more pussy juice from his slave. My ass hurt so much now though that I couldn't cum and was grateful that nobody ordered me to. Master had his fill and now sat down in front of me pushing his cock into my mouth. I immediately sucked away on it for all I was worth. In the meantime, Master Alex had exchanged the paddle for a strap and my beating once again continued, though not as hard out of respect for my master who had his cock in my mouth. SMACK, SMACK, BAM, WHACK, WHACK. *"Owww"* I began letting out a continuous muffled scream. The blows came down very fast. Master Alex was not messing around, but still I had to force myself to pleasure my master or the beating would never end. I sucked on my owner's cock as hard as I could, forcing my mind to concentrate on just that, not my scalding ass. *WHACK, WHACK, BAM, BAM, CRACK, CRACK.* Both masters were clearly getting so much pleasure from my ordeal that I could not tell when it would stop. Just then master Alex stopped and went and got the sorority paddle, the big one with holes in it. "And for the finale, ten of my best." My master took his cock out of my mouth and sat back contentedly watching. "Count them out slave." BAM" *"Ahhhh, one sir."* BAM *" Oww two sir."* SMACK *"owww three sir."* I was crying hard now and even when the paddle wasn't landing on my ass it still hurt. It all felt like one continuous intense spanking. I kept counting out the blows though and finally they ended but my crying continued on. I pulled on my bonds, and as usual that did no good. I would continue crying for thirty minutes after the spanking ended. Both masters sat down and chatted, very impressed with themselves. In time I heard Master Alex get up. I looked back and watched him lube up my anus. He then made himself hard and entered me in it.

Master Alex grabbed me by the sides and pounded me from the gitgo. It would keep me crying but soon, gratefully, a wave of pleasure rolled over me and I begged for permission to cum. My master allowed it. Wow did I ever need that. With my ass so sore, sorer than it's ever been, I needed to get my mind on something else. My owner came over and once again stuck his cock in my mouth. I sucked as hard as I could. Master then unstrapped my wrists so I could play with his balls. I concentrated on my master' cock, sucking as hard as I could. I was now cumming hard and not concerned about my scalding ass.

I don't know how long all that lasted but in time there was no cock in my ass and my owner went back to my pussy for a reload of my pussy juice. I hope I once again was giving him all he wanted but I don't really know. I was left there exhausted and limp as the both masters got dressed and chatted. I heard something about me but couldn't make it out. My master came over and unstrapped me and ordered me into the big cage were I obediently went, rubbing my ass furiously. I looked back at my ass after I was locked securely in the cage and saw it was dark red with more marks. Tell me I didn't really have 2 more spankings to go. This was definitely the day from hell. Both masters went upstairs and left me naked with my thoughts and well-beaten ass.

Chapter Eight

The best I could do was lie down on my stomach in the cage. Sitting was no longer an option. I hoped that one of my next beatings would be on my tits as they were in less pain than my ass. Soon master came down, opened the cage and ordered me to make dinner. I had stopped crying and was ready for a change of venue. I was ordered to stop as I walked by so he could rub my scorching ass. "Wow" he exclaimed. "I don't think I've ever seen it like this." "It hurts terribly master. Please no more. I have learned my lesson I swear." I did really feel I had learned my lesson. "Come up with me and I'll put some cream on it to dull the pain" he said. Wow, that sounded good. I followed master up the stairs. "Go wait for me by the couch." I knelt down on my knees on the carpet by the couch. I kept my very tender ass in the air. Master came back and ordered me across his lap, as if he was going to spank me. He commenced to rub a pain killing lotion onto my ass. Nice. It would take about 20 minutes for its full impact but after being sent to the kitchen to fix dinner, I really felt it kick in and oh what a relief it was. This would definitely help me get through my next two spankings. Man I wonder who they would be by? I could also hope that master would be concerned and cancel them, or at least one of them.

My master was in the living room drinking a glass of wine. Master Alex had left a while back. I poked my head into the living room and asked "Master do I really need any more spankings today?" He smiled and said "yes you do young lady, but I will be giving both of them to you." I think that was good. At least I knew his style better and he would look out for me more than the others, so yes that's good. As I turned to leave he said. "The last spanking of the night will be your bedtime spanking but the second to the last you can choose. It can be spanking your tits, or your ass. You think about which you'd prefer." "Yes sir." Well the answer was easy, spank my tits. They didn't hurt as much and hopefully I could get some pleasure from it. I started to walk back into the kitchen and turned and walked back into the living room, blurting out "spank my tits please sir." "Very well."

I fixed meat loaf, rice, carrots and made a salad. I put my inflatable ring pillow on my seat at the dinner table and gratefully master didn't mind. During dinner, amazingly my spankings never came up. We made small talk. I cleared the table, cleaned the dishes and went out to the living room to watch TV in master' arms. I was naked of course as master was.

It was about 7:30 and master kissed me on the lips and said it was time for my tits to get the required attention. I said yes sir and dragged myself up. "You pick what I shall use on them and come here with it." "Yes sir" I said obediently. I went to the closet of implements and looked around. Well gee, from experience I knew the suede slapper hurt my ass the least so let's try that. I brought it to master who was sitting on the edge of the couch smiling. He had rope with him and ordered me to sit on the carpet in front of him with my hands behind my back. I forced myself to sit on my butt, he then tied my wrists together so they'd be behind my back and out of the way.

To my surprise master then ordered me to stand up and sit on the couch, but directly in front of him, (thus I would be on the same level as him.) He took out lotion and before I knew it my breasts were getting massaged like Master Alex had earlier. At first they were sensitive from the whippings of the day but the pain subsided and turned into some type of painful pleasure. I cooed and rubbed my back seductively up against my master's chest as waves of pleasure emanated from my breasts. They were always so sensitive and master loved them. It took me longer than usual but I finally asked for permission to cum. I came quietly. Master would concentrate on the nipples for a while, running his well lubricated fingers quickly in circles around them, then pull back to knead and massage all of both breasts, while trying not to touch the nipples. Then all of a sudden he would furiously twist around the more sensitive and now very slippery nipples, which would make me explode with pleasure. Master went on and on with this and I kept cumming for him, admittedly not my hardest orgasms of the day but a very welcome sensation. Then master pulled me out of my haze by stopping. He cleaned his hands and my tits off with a cloth that he had handy, then he ordered me to sit with my back to him on the carpet just below him. Sitting was still a tough experience but I had the pillow under me which helped. Master pulled my head back towards his lap and ordered me to keep it there so as to have a better spanking angle on my breasts. He took up the slapper and ran it over my breasts for some time, massaging them with it. I quivered in anticipation. Then the spanks started but only light ones and they stayed light for some time, though progressively getting stronger. Master concentrated spanking both nipples, but clearly this was meant not to be a hard spanking. I had gotten lucky. Master would grab a nipple and pull the breast up and out, that way it gave him more tit to spank. He did this with both breasts several times. With the breast pulled out by the nipple, he would concentrate spanking its lower breast, then both sides of that breast and then the upper breast. Clearly master was really enjoying himself. My tits were already rather red and this made them redder. I did hurt though as they were already beaten hard twice today. After 100 or so light to moderate spanks to my tits, it was over. Master untied me, turned me around and pulled me over for a kiss. He sat me next to him for more cuddling and TV. He did warn me though that my last spanking of the day, my bedtime spanking, would be a hard one and that I would cry myself to sleep tonight.

Chapter Nine

As master and I shared some quiet time together on the couch, he had me suck on his cock for around 15 minutes. He was particularly horny that day as I've noted. He later had me get down on the carpet in front of him. He then tied my wrists together behind my back, then had me kneel in front of him so he could more readily play with my breasts. He would reach down from time to time to massage and lightly spank my upturned bottom with a long 5 gallon bucket paint stirring stick. He wasn't spanking hard at the moment but I knew that would come later, and sure enough it did. Master provided me with a good helping of his delicious ooze. Then he ordered me to get back on my knees in front of him and gave me a loving kiss. He then told me that the finale of the day was at hand. He untied my wrists, I was then ordered to get ready for bed. My instructions were to lay face down on my belly waiting for my 10th and final spanking of the day. I had butterflies in my stomach because I knew how hard this spanking would be. Still I was grateful that I had had so much pleasure that day and also had provided others, particularly my wonderful master, so much pleasure. Still I knew what was coming up would be really tough and I knew master wanted it to be that painful so I would cry myself to sleep. Knowing that such a severe spanking was eminent in a way was good because I would know not to hold back and to instead start crying as early as I wanted too.

I did my nighttime routine and told master I was ready for bed. Master ordered me to kneel in front of him so he could tie my hands together in front of me. I was naked as usual, now with my hands tied in front of me. I got onto the bed on my stomach and waited for what was sure to be a very painful experience.

I was genuinely scared and quite unexpectedly I started to cry while just waiting for this terrible punishment. Master came in with a strap and a paddle. He sat down next to me and began sternly lecturing me. He was clearly working himself up to do something sadistic. I apologized profusely for being forgetful as I was crying already out of fear. Master put a timer on the headboard in front of me and informed me that this spanking would last 20 minutes and would be hard. He then began spanking me.

I would cry the entire time. Master doesn't usually spank me with his hand but today was an unusual day in many respects. SMACK, SMACK, BAM, WHACK, WHACK. *"Owww"* I let myself go and cried with abandon, more than I really needed. I had really let my master down and I deserved this punishment, I knew that. His blows came down very fast. CRACK, CRACK, BAM, BAM, BAM, WHAP, WHAP. "I am absolutely not accepting your forgetfulness anymore and will happily have it beaten out of you." *"Owww, yesss sir, oh, pleassee noo more."* SMACK, BAM, WHACK, CRACK, CRACK, BAM. Master then went back and forth spanking each cheek as hard as he could for around 5 minutes. He was genuinely upset. Then he stopped. He tied my bound hands to the bed headboard and tied each leg to a corner bed post. I would now be a particularly easy target as it would be so difficult for me to move away from the blows. He took up the strap and without hesitation once again began beating. *"Nooo ohh...masters....oww...ahhh...ahhh."* My ass was once again on fire and really hurting. I was hoping it would turn me on enough to cum but no way. WHAP, WHAP, WHAP, CRACK. He apparently grew tired for the moment of beating my ass and used the strap on my upper thighs, now grunting at times as he laid down the blows. I was no longer feeling the individual spanks as much and instead it all melded into one continuous wave of pain. I tried to turn my ass away from the blows but the combination of his strong grip and the tight bondage made that impossible. He continued to lay it on my ass with abandon. WHACK, WHACK, CRACK, WHAP. *"Ow, ohhh, owww, no, pleaseee..ahhhh."* I bent my head back and clenched my buttcheeks with all my might but it did no good. Master was hell bent on taking care of this problem once and for all.

This spanking no doubt hurt worse thanks to all the spankings I already had. I was laying on my sore tits but quickly I would not even be feeling their soreness, even though I was rubbing them against the sheets as I wiggled back and forth. CRACK, WHAP, WHAP, SLAP, WHAP. My crying was uncontrollable now and bordered on a wail. This is what my master wanted. This was a big time spanking that we would talk about for years to come and that he would threaten me with if I was bad. *"Owww, no, ahhhh, stoppp pleassee."* It went on and on and master was breathing heavy now, still angrily scolding me off and on but I could no longer tell what he was saying. My mind was in a heavily spanked haze. I didn't dare look at my ass but I knew this would leave lots of marks and sitting would be difficult for many days. SMACK, SMACK, CRACK, WHAP, WHAP. I kicked my feet as much as I could with them being tied down. I kept clenching my cheeks but when I would do that master would beat the cheeks harder. Then he stopped but I knew it was just to get the paddle for the last round of this nightmare. I would never be forgetful, I just couldn't go through this again. I must work harder. Master grabbed me around the waist once again and without a word began where he left off. Now the blows from the paddle were aimed for the top of the left cheek, where it meets the back and steadily landing further and further down until 30 or so spanks later it was on the middle thigh. He then did the same to the right cheek. I had lost touch with space and time and was crying like a schoolgirl. I don't remember what I said as I pleaded for him to stop. Fortunately, the timer began ringing and the spanking was over.

Master threw down the paddle and got up and walked off. I lay there tied down and sobbing. *"I'llll never dooo it again."* I promised. I wanted so badly to rub my ass but couldn't as I was tied down so securely. Unfortunately for me the torment continued as my ass was in so much pain. 10 minutes later I tried to stop crying but couldn't. 30 minutes later master would come back with the pain killing lotion and sit down beside me. I pleaded for his forgiveness. He rubbed my bottom lovingly. "I do this because I love you sweetheart." I tried to thank him but was having too much trouble talking. I managed to mumble something. Master rubbed the painkilling lotion onto my cheeks and untied my legs, which I instinctively kicked up and down, though that would do no good. My hands however he left tied knowing that now I still couldn't rub my cheeks, which was something I wanted to do so badly. He pulled the covers over me, kissed my cheek and left the room, leaving me alone with my thoughts and incredibly sore ass. I kept on crying and sure enough cried myself to sleep.

The End